T0329216

Cambridge Elements ☰

Elements in Religion and Violence
edited by
James R. Lewis
University of Tromsø
and
Margo Kitts
Hawai'i Pacific University

ELEMENTS OF
RITUAL AND VIOLENCE

Margo Kitts
Hawai'i Pacific University

CAMBRIDGE
UNIVERSITY PRESS

CAMBRIDGE
UNIVERSITY PRESS

University Printing House, Cambridge CB2 8BS, United Kingdom

One Liberty Plaza, 20th Floor, New York, NY 10006, USA

477 Williamstown Road, Port Melbourne, VIC 3207, Australia

314–321, 3rd Floor, Plot 3, Splendor Forum, Jasola District Centre,
New Delhi – 110025, India

79 Anson Road, #06–04/06, Singapore 079906

Cambridge University Press is part of the University of Cambridge.

It furthers the University's mission by disseminating knowledge in the pursuit of
education, learning, and research at the highest international levels of excellence.

www.cambridge.org
Information on this title: www.cambridge.org/9781108448321
DOI: 10.1017/9781108692236

First published 2018

A catalogue record for this publication is available from the British Library.

ISBN 978-1-108-44832-1 Paperback
ISSN 2397-9496 (online)
ISSN 2514-3786 (print)

Cambridge Elements

Elements of Ritual and Violence

Margo Kitts

Hawai'i Pacific University

ABSTRACT: Ritualized violence is by definition not haphazard or random, but seemingly intentional and often ceremonial. It has a long history in religious practice, as attested in texts and artifacts from the earliest civilizations. It is equally evident in the behaviors of some contemporary religious activists and within initiatory practices ongoing in many regions of the world. Given its longevity and cultural expanse, ritualized violence presumably exerts a pull deeply into the sociology, psychology, anthropology, theology, and perhaps even ontology of its practitioners, but this is not transparent. This short volume sketches the subject of ritualized violence. That is, it summarizes some established theories about ritual and about violence, and ponders a handful of striking instantiations of their link.

KEYWORDS: ritual, violence, body, menace

ISBNs: 9781108448321 (PB), 9781108692236 (OC)

DOI: 10.1017/9781108692236

Contents

Ritualized Violence: Why Does It Matter?

Ritualized violence is by definition not haphazard or random, but seemingly intentional and often ceremonial. It has a long history in religious practice, as attested in texts and artifacts from the earliest civilizations. It is equally evident in the behaviors of some contemporary religious activists and within initiatory practices ongoing in many regions of the world. Given its longevity and cultural expanse, ritualized violence presumably exerts a pull deeply into the sociology, psychology, anthropology, theology, perhaps even ontology of its practitioners, but this is not transparent. This short volume will sketch the subject of ritualized violence. That is, it will summarize some established theories about ritual and about violence, and will ponder a handful of striking instantiations of their links.

As will be shown, the meanings of both ritual and violence may be contested, and the link between them need not be presumed. However, the worthiness of studying their conceivable link when there is one, can be supported by a glance at two famous examples, one ancient and one contemporary. Consider, first, why it is mandated that the Israelites who took Jericho were to commit themselves to Joshua to the death (Josh 1:17), consecrate themselves (3:5), circumcise themselves (5:3), and march around Jericho seven times on the seventh day blowing horns and shouting (6:15–17), before the walls fell and they laid siege to the city and "destroyed with the sword every living thing in it – men and women, young and old, cattle, sheep and donkeys" (6:21[1]). That is, how did the initial buildup to the destruction prepare, if it did, people to destroy and also bear on the felt significance of that destruction? Contextual differences notwithstanding, why is it also that the 9/11 perpetrators swore oaths to die, sanctified themselves bodily (by bathing, shaving, applying cologne, arranging clothing), prayed and recited verses

---

[1] The New International Version of the Bible (NIV) has been used throughout.

of the Qur'an, even expectorated those verses onto clothing, passports, and papers, and shouted before performing the final events which resulted in the collapse of New York's twin towers, the wounding of the Pentagon, an airplane crash into a field in Pennsylvania, and the deaths of nearly 3,000 people?[2] These presteps, prescribed in the 9/11 Last Instructions, similarly to the steps described in the biblical book of Joshua, impel us to contemplate the formalized nature of certain destructive acts. Quite aside from whatever rhetorical purpose these documents may have served (e.g., prescriptive? commemorative? propagandistic? fanciful?), they force us to ponder what ritualization might be expected to add, if anything, for the actors who perpetrated the violence. Even if the lists of preparations were merely hyperbolic and/or immaterial to the actual motives of violent actors, we still are impelled to consider the intended effects of imagined behaviors, and why the behaviors were captured in texts.

Of course, precisely because the above rituals were captured as texts, we must grapple with the matter of evidence, an enduring problem in ritual studies. What kind of evidence provides a window into the actual experience of ritual practitioners? With all the complexities of even identifying a ritual these days, most scholars do accept that something is being experienced and communicated via a bodily event which is not quite casual and which occurs in space and time. Whether or not experience of that event can be captured entirely in texts is disputable. The problem is greater than discerning the experiential realities behind scribal propaganda. Rather, textualization brings with it an intrinsic problem, namely the extent to which discursive reasoning – arguments in language – may capture and represent a ritual's full sensory dimensions.

For instance, how exhaustively may discursive reasoning capture and represent experiences of rhythm, heat, pain, or pleasure, and, for that matter, delight or disgust? For ancient rituals, unfortunately, discursive representation as

---

[2] Analyzed in Kitts (2010).

captured in texts constitutes the bulk of our evidence. Although we do have a few ritual scenes inscribed in art,[3] some suggestive votive offerings, and ancient Near Eastern figurines concealed within foundation deposits (presumably part of a ritual), the significance of such artifacts is not transparent.[4] Provocative as the documents and artifacts may be, we can get an important sense of what this evidence does *not* capture by glancing at perplexed reports from contemporary ethnographers, who sometimes hit a wall when it comes to grasping visceral ritual experiences such as trance, mind-altering pain, or the ecstatic visions of the living ritual practitioners whom ethnographers study.[5] Beyond the hurdle of translating bodily events into language, there is also the problem of tracing the bodily events' impact, if any, into subsequent feeling or behavior. If we cannot conceptually grasp the full experience of the ritual, how do we conceptually trace its full dynamism into social and personal realities? These issues obviously bear on analysis of any ritual, but include rituals enmeshed with violence.

As an object of study, violence is equally enigmatic. Consider the range of possible meanings for the term "violence." Inflictions of bodily pain or death are straightforward enough, but consider too implied threats (e.g., military displays, menacing postures, manipulation of threatening symbols), rude gestures, verbal abuse, social suppressions and disciplinary behaviors, ceremonial maiming (e.g., scarification, circumcision, finger severing), desecrations of holy sites, agonistic sports, outright war, even restrictive categorizations: the possibilities seem endless! The problem is not simply a matter of violence being

---

[3] Collon (2003) analyzes ancient Near Eastern dancing scenes, for instance.

[4] The early materials are increasingly rich, though. See studies by, e.g., Bahrani 2008; Collon 2003; Thomas 2012; Insoll 2013.

[5] Ethnomusicologists offer wonderful bridge-views, some by allowing themselves to experience first-hand the rhythms and sensations of ritual participation, and then attempting to capture those sensations in discursive analysis. See Friedson (1996, 2009) and Becker (2004).

in the eye of the beholder. In the ritual context, there is also the problem of locating the violence. That is, what appear to be ritualized acts of violence may generate effects which are not perceivably violent at all or, alternatively, violence may be an indirect result of seemingly innocuous ritual behavior. For instance, a ritual which involves bodily maiming, a seemingly violent act, might generate identity and belonging within a group whose aims are quite pacific, whereas seemingly nonviolent ritual behaviors such as chanting or dancing may bind group members together closely enough to provide a social foundation for outwardly aggressive acts.

The enigma of locating the violence extends to certain political acts which arguably are ritualized. Public executions, for instance, have been argued to be formally staged in such a way as to capture the public imagination and to insinuate sovereign force over not only the executed, but also the witnessing audience (Foucault 1977:3–8). Military marches presumably may arouse similar trepidation or, equally, enthusiasm; the mesh of nationalist and religious fervor, served by prayer, proclamation, and ceremony, has received a great deal of study: strategy and ceremony are not easy to disentangle in some instances.[6] The same may be said of self-damaging displays, such as campaigns of fasting and self-immolation (conceived as necroresistance by Bargu (2014), among others). These may rely on ancient ritual prototypes for form, but also may be geared toward swaying popular opinion against dominant regimes, as we have seen in Turkey, Tibet, Ireland, and elsewhere. However traditional, body-damaging displays may rivet attention and generate discomfort for witnesses, relating to what Morgan has explored as the haptic dimension of imagination (2012). At the same time they may arouse anguish and outrage, and impel political resistance.

---

[6] See, e.g., Bobič (2012), Hutchinson (2009), and, classically, Kertzer (1996/1988).

As we shall see, violence can have so many different expressions that the meaning of the term is increasingly elusive. As a brief introduction to the academic study of both violence and ritual, this volume begins with the problem of defining violence, and follows by attempting to pin down ritual. Peppering the discussion are examples which illustrate the complexities. An excursus on the cognitive science of ritual concludes Section II. The third section offers a brief exploration of the communicational dynamic of rituals whose overt intent is menace.

Section I: Violence

We begin with the truism that violence, ritualized or not, is in the eye of the beholder. The problem is not simply that one person's violent act is another's heroic feat, but also that seemingly violent acts are often mini-steps within larger strategies for which violence is acknowledged obliquely, if at all. As described in this section, the conceivable ways of imagining, symbolizing, and staging violence are profuse.

Consider, first, the immediate consequences of physical violence – presumably pain, death, or damaged bodily integrity. These are not monolithic in the way they are perceived across cultures. The experience of pain may be repulsive and power-sapping to some, but transforming, empowering, even rapturous to others. As Glucklich has described, this is particularly so for certain members of the religious who seek sacred pain through practices of self-harm (2003:79–105). Pain may have functional value in initiation rituals. It has been argued that pain may be instrumental in flattening realities (Scarry 1987:11, 27, 202) as well as in constructing them, even conferring a quality of "incontestable reality" on that power that has brought pain into being (Beidelman 1997:179; Morinis 1985:166–168). As we shall see, painful ordeals may result in the stunning annihilation of previously received truths, as well as in epiphanies of new ones. The dynamic quality of pain is a peculiar feature of many religious practices.

A similar elasticity may apply to notions of violent death. Musing on Simone Weil's famous "The Iliad, or the Poem of Force," Sontag observed that violent death is perspectival: for Weil it makes bodies into things, but for others it makes martyrs and heroes (Sontag 2003:13). We hear endlessly that Americans fear both pain and death, whereas martyrs for various causes seek those experiences (Cook 2007), even when pain and death bring no ostensible heavenly reward, as among the Liberation Tigers of Tamil Elam (LTTE) (Schalk 2010). Memorial tributes to the violently dead (such as murals of martyrs, walls of names, mounds of skulls or eyeglasses), as well as commemorative performances (such as passion plays, eulogies, poems), may be said to defeat the finality of death in the hearts and memories of a beholden public.[7] Then there is an added complexity when death is seen not as instantaneous, but rather as an extended process lasting for months or years, and ritually demarcated at intervals along the way (Shimazono and Kitts 2013). Thus, death's very definition may be socially circumscribed.

Bodily integrity, likewise, is socially and also personally circumscribed. At the simplest level, one person's bodily mutilation or scarification is another person's badge of identity or of beauty, and probably has been so since our first self-decorating ancestors (Schildkrout 2004; Bahn 1998:70–81). Beyond the issue of painful rites, skin itself increasingly is scrutinized as an interstitial thing. Skin-marking or altering is said to speak to the fleshiness of intercorporeality (Ahmed and Stacey 2001; Shildrick 2001:11), as not exclusively about projecting outward an internal self, but rather as reflecting the porosity between inner and outer and between oneself and others. Donna Haraway has challenged not only bodily but also species autonomy, preferring instead to

---

[7] See Kitts, ed., for an array of religious perspectives on martyrdom (2018).

examine the intersectionality among ourselves and other creatures at the level of inter-species engagement, even at the level of the colonizing bacteria in our bodies and the evolutionary feat of symbiogenesis (2006).[8] New and exciting rubrics have been launched to ponder fleshly experience and modification (e.g., tattooing, artificial limbs, transplants, sexual reassignment). Disputes about alterity, hybridity, and monstrosity characterize an emerging discourse about the body, in art, religion, and bioethics.

Beyond the level of philosophical inquiry, there is the more ethnographic matter of varying historical perspectives and social contexts for pain and bodily integrity. The problems may be illustrated by a glance at the initiation rituals among Mende secret societies during the civil conflicts in Sierra Leone in the 1990s. Charged with defending their communities against the Revolutionary United Front (RUF), the Mende's Kamajors, or hunters, were initiated into their defensive roles by methods that a Westerner might deem painful, distressing to bodily integrity, or even viscerally repulsive. By rumor, Kamajors ritually cut initiands' bodies, applied immunizing potions to the cuts – thereby inducing scarification – supervised initiands' consumption of concoctions containing human tissues or organs, and dressed them in clothing and artifacts constructed by ritual means. These last included specialized jackets, masks, charms, and amulets made of severed body parts. For the Kamajors, the cutting and scarring, reputed cannibalism, and wearing of corporeal amulets were explained by traditional invincibility metaphors: the goal of the rituals was not pain, damage, or shock, but rather empowerment and transformation (Wlodarzcyk 2009:27–49, 81–91; Ellis 1995). Successful initiands were thought to repel bullets and to defy gravity. As Richards put it, they were "dressed to kill," that is, transformed and committed (2009). Their less traditional opponents simulated these same practices with concocted ritual expressions and invocations of obscure spiritual authorities.

---

[8] Overarching summary provided by Vasquez (2011:165–169).

As Wlodarczyk notes, Kamajor strategies were persuasive on the battlefield. Not only the practices but also the rumors of the practices intimidated opponents, thereby resulting in concrete effects (2009:83–91). Thus, while the violence in these practices was not ignored by practitioners, it was subsumed within strategies of immunization against wounds and of fortification of defensive powers, to which their opponents gave witness. The violence, if acknowledged at all, resonated in terms shaped by tradition.

In the contemporary West, the subject of violence is highlighted in both popular and scholarly discourses. Popular thinking has tended to consign violent acts to outbreaks of anarchy, primitive atavism, social contagion, personal disengagement and the like, while some social scientists and religious historians now contemplate the possibly constitutive roles of staged violence in social institutions and religious imagination. The subject is vast.[9] The discussion that follows sketches violence in popular imagination and social experience, then in theories based in anthropology and religious performance, and finally as a perennial product of human societies, according to some theorists.

Popular Perspectives on Violence and Its Effects

It has been claimed that popular conceptions of violence, as presented in the media and casual discourse, eschew outbreaks of violence as wild, meaningless, a fall into chaos or immorality, and in need of suppression or redirection by the totality of society (Whitehead 2007:40; Aijmer 2000:1). But much is left out of these conceptions, even within the arena of popular opinion. First, on the largest scale, the last century's ethnocides, the way they are memorialized, and their lingering psychodynamics among victims and perpetrators are anything

---

[9] On the link of violence with religion in its myriad manifestations, see Juergensmeyer, Kitts, and Jerryson, eds (2013). See Juergensmeyer and Kitts, eds (2011), for excerpts of theories from traditional scholars on the subject.

but meaningless, as the psychologists of collective trauma have taught us (e.g., Volkan et al., 2002); rather, they shape consciousness and culture in a variety of ways for generations to come. It would be frivolous to downplay the real as well as the cultural consequences of campaigns of destruction conducted on a state or societal scale. Symbolizations of such campaigns dot the public landscape as poignant reminders of wartime cruelties. Skull racks from Rwanda and Cambodia; murals of martyrs in Egypt, the Philippines, and elsewhere; concentration camp memorials from World War II; the 9/11 wall of names; and other shrines to victims of violence are conspicuous features not only of the public landscape, but also of public memory. Such exhibits resound with meanings. Presumably pacific by design, they also inflame anguish and enmity and precipitate calls for revenge, while at the same time offering sites for pilgrimage and public grief. Memorials are represented not only by shrines, of course, but also by performances. Song, drama, dance, art, and poetry venerate the fallen, as they have done since the time of the Homeric epics. Arguably, in this era of global media and public memorials, popular awareness is more informed than ever before about human-on-human violence.

At the same time, the plenum of violent spectacles in popular culture has also spurred a trend to reflect upon and to decry our obsession with the staging of violence in art and media. Some, with Baudrillard (2002), attribute our hunger for such spectacles to nostalgia for an irrecoverable dimension of "the real." By this postmodernist theory, twenty-first-century consciousness is hit by a numbing blitzkrieg of media-based, violent simulacra – not just photos and memorials, but violent simulations in the form of games, dystopic novels, horror films, and trauma art. Our attention yanked from one spectacle to another, we reputedly stare at violent spectacles because we crave a sensuous connection with things that has been lost. Trauma art has become infamous as the new ritual stage. As Siebers argued, by staring at mangled, lifeless bodies, we search for aesthetic meanings which reach beyond the plain fact of death or mutilation; instead, the altered, damaged, or dead body becomes a hyper-canvas for contemplating the significances we once pondered through religious stories and rituals (2003). Historians of Near Eastern antiquity will attest that such hyper-canvases, whereon the specter of bodily mangling is highlighted, are not recent, but rather millennia old.[10] Nonetheless, in this era of bloody videogames, ISIS beheading videos, and snuff films, Siebers's point about the present-day fascination with trauma art is an indisputable one.

Yet, over the past few decades some have proffered counterarguments, claiming that contemporary audiences find spectacles of violence and its effects not fascinating, but rather routine, boring, even conducive to an incipient sadism. Repeated artistic fixations on the impact of violence are said have rendered violent images inauthentic, "bleached" of the potential to inspire horror (Sontag 2003:64). This is said to be the case especially for young viewers who increasingly are inured to the suffering of others. For them, reputedly, violent images have lost their punch. World War II atrocity photos, thus, are said to have completed their vital role of testifying to human cruelty, and now are dismissed as banal, maudlin, even as kitsch. At worst they revivify the gaze of violent perpetrators (Crane 2008), rather than advance the identities of the victims whose personhoods were lost. The 2004 Abu Ghraib photos have been said to rivet our attention not so much for the captured spectacle of human suffering – we see no faces, not in the human pyramid nor in the hooded man – but for their windows into the prison guards' imaginations and the staging of aberrant art (Binder 2010). Giroux notes a similar depravity of aesthetics in the 2010 "kill team photos" from Afghanistan. In Giroux's view, the photos were, among other things, icons of a subculture of sadist cruelty, fed by a commercially fanned death drive (2011).

---

[10] And typically associated with royal and/or divine terror and sovereignty. See Bahrani (2008), Noegel (2007), and Kitts (2017b).

Still others, though, see this popular numbing to violence as incomplete, and the moods inspired by violent spectacles as richly ambiguous. Religious audiences, in particular, seem to preserve an age-old taste for the beautification of suffering and mutilation, as is clear in representations of tortured Christian saints (Eco 2007:56–61) or of martyrs in the Middle East (Khosronejad 2012). Chronicling the history of our fascination with war photography and touching upon the iconography of religious suffering, Sontag pointed to viewing such spectacles as a guilty pleasure (2003:61, 86): "There is the satisfaction of being able to look at the image without flinching. There is the pleasure of flinching" (2003:34). In her view, although we can get habituated to images of suffering, habituation is not automatic, even – or especially – when suffering is tied to familiar narratives. Representations of the crucifixion do not become banal to Christian believers, the staged martyrdom and beheading of Hussein do not fail to move Shiites, and performances of the Chushingura, a war tale dramatized in many media, still evoke tears from Japanese audiences: "They weep, in part, because they have seen it many times. People want to weep. Pathos, in the form of a narrative, does not wear out" (Sontag 2003:65). Plus, such images are polyvocal: "Photographs of the suffering and martyrdom of a people are more than reminders of death, of failure, of victimization. They invoke the miracle of survival ... People want to be able to visit – and refresh – their memories" (2003:69). All of this is to argue that the violence staged in spectacles may wield a powerful impact on imagination after all, especially when viewers recognize the figures violated and impute existential salience to their sufferings.[11]

Of course, nonreligiously identified audiences too can experience a painful sympathy with dead or mutilated figures, even with violent actors, before popular media have assigned the figure a trope. Contemplating the 2003

---

[11] On Iranian martyrdom and the different manipulations of the suffering trope, see Partow (2014) and Khosronejad (2012).

photograph of the upper torso of a Chechen suicide bomber in Moscow, Vikki Bell observes the arousal of an immediate and distinct kind of foreboding which is personalized in the viewer's body; simultaneously, it is startling to the imagination and ineptly politicized in public discourse (2005). Viewing the young woman's face and intact torso, Bell observed the conundrum created by the fleeting awareness of a life-in-common (that of the bomber and her witnesses) conjoined with an existential realization of life's puniness (so easily snuffed out) along with a discourse about the suicide in a politicized register, a rational register – e.g., why she did it. The conundrum is jarring, to say the least. For Bell, such is the effect of suicide bombing. We respond in horror not only to the belittling of our life-in-common and the seemingly secondary nature of any intended political discourse, but also to a kind of sublime transcendence based on, in Bell's terms, the self's own "rational capacity to grasp the infinite, supersensible purposiveness to nature" (2005:254), by which she seems to mean the hard fact of human mortality. In any case, since there is no actor left to articulate the meaning of her death, it is the lingering spectacle that generates mood and sways imagination. By this way of thinking, the spectacularization of violence can shoot emotional trajectories into different spheres of experience, and unevenly so.[12]

Violence in Philosophical–Anthropological Discourse

The trajectories in which violence penetrates popular imagination may be approached from perspectives outside of art and media, of course. Perhaps most radically, Nigel Rapport ponders social violence in the form of discursive alterity. In this view, democratic violence – creative, alternative postulations which disrupt ordinary assumptions and promote new understandings – is to be

---

[12] If the effects can be captured in narrative at all. See Benjamin (1986 [1921]) and Michelsen (2015:92–94), contra Fierke (2013).

distinguished from nihilistic violence – alternative postulations intended to unsettle and disorientate, to breach the surface of civil exchange (2000:53). Rapport's is not a new observation. Nietzsche and Sartre too addressed the self-inventing violence of humans, who are born into constraining social and economic contexts but able to imagine and actualize their ways out of them. Conceivably, both disturbing and creative forms of violence are constants in human discourse, reflecting a perennial instability but also dynamism in social processes. As Rapport points out, our capacity for self-invention is tied essentially to imagination, as the gratuitous bursting forth that enables individuals to transcend the contexts into which they were born (2000:39–54). This capacity to invent ourselves anew may be regarded as inherently conflictual, since our talent for self-fictionalization inevitably collides with seemingly fixed social structures and natural processes. In this way of thinking, some form of violence may occur inexorably at the juncture of self and world, manifest when the self attempts to shake off and subvert a received identity.

Also pondering the juncture of self and world is the layered, symbological approach to violent imagination offered by Göran Aijmer (2000). Conjoining "cultural semantics, social pragmatics, and operational functions," Aijmer observes that violence has several natures, three of which involve iconic, discursive, and ethological "orders" of human experience (2000:2). Perhaps the most intriguing order is iconic, by which he means a dimension of imagination which eludes identification in ordinary discourse but whose images "make manifest people's intuitive cognizance as to what ultimately conditions social and personal experience" (2000:3). This iconic order, comprised of "symbolic displays of strong expressive force, yet ... working outside language ... and thus without referential meaning" (2000:3), can be instrumental in envisioning, building, altering, even threatening possible worlds. Its effect is all the more powerful because it can elude discourse. The second order is precisely discursive, and so involves verbal articulations and "the intentional performative acts of men and women of a society, and their ongoing conversation about themselves and the world" (2000:4). The iconic and discursive orders, as Aijmer sees it, are constrained ultimately by the ethological order, which is based on the fact that "human activities have a biological/genetic dimension" which involves the "complex processes of thinking and remembering" and our susceptibility to pain and death (2000:4). I have argued elsewhere that these orders intertwine, as they did when the United States was presented with the famous photo of the hooded prisoner teetering on a box at Abu Ghraib. The ambiguous crucifixion imagery (iconic dimension) immediately eclipsed the ethological and discursive dimensions (his fear of pain or death was invisible to us; we were initially speechless), but eventually spurred a discussion about martyrdom, torture, and aberrant art (Kitts 2013a:418; Binder 2010). Beyond the United States, these iconic displays of violence, educing more than the ethological reality of pain and death, conceivably assumed socio-symbolic significance in launching revenge and a discourse about martyrdom, all at the same time. Aijmer's approach is significant because it addresses the layered dimensions of our responses to violence. The different layers may not be equally conspicuous to us at any one time.

Of course, this tendency to adduce to human experience layers too deep for formalization in discourse has occupied theorists at least since the existential phenomenologists (e.g., Merleau-Ponty 1962; Heidegger 1962), and, for that matter, probably since Freud's *Totem and Taboo* (1946 [1918]). In religious and anthropological theories, pre-articulate experiences generated by violence have tended to cluster around suffering, terror, and pain – all constituting a kind of trauma. Suffering, for instance, is said to be irreducibly present to consciousness – like color or sound – but at the same time to resist one's ability to express and convey it fully; ritualization has been argued to give it partial voice (Seeman 2005, discussing Levinas, Weber, and Geertz). Terror, in the sense of bodily (virtual) contingency in a world riddled with unpredictability, has been associated with a sick dread of imminent annihilation since Freud's essay on the uncanny (1919) and Otto's on the holy (1958 [1917]). Religious literature and poetry seem to fixate on the theme precisely because terror is existentially transformative and, at the same time, evasive to conceptual capture.[13] Lastly, intense physical pain is said to elude language and to resist integration into personal narratives (Scarry 1987), yet to be a powerful mnemonic device for creating context and anchoring signification (Crapanzano 2004:89–93). All of these experiences have titillated scholarly imaginations, but particularly the imaginations of anthropologists and those religious theorists who focus on performative violence.

Some Anthropological Perspectives on Pain and Trauma

Anthropological field work and comparative studies support the deeply rooted and perspective-altering nature of trauma and pain (e.g., Morinis 1985, Beidelman 1997, Glucklich 2003), particularly in relation to socially sanctioned violence. The theories of Bloch (1992), Whitehouse (2004), and Alcorta and Sosis (2013) crystallize some major themes.

Bloch sees trauma as a pivot for social transformation. Two of Bloch's examples are the Orokaiva of Papua New Guinea and the Dinka of South Sudan. As he sees it, Orokaiva children undergo initiatory experiences in which they are made to experience a terrifying closeness first to victims destined for sacrifice (pigs, as symbolic prey), and then to overcome that closeness by identifying with ancestral bird-spirits (symbolic hunters), who have just hunted and killed the prey with whom the children first identified. Having killed the prey (their former near-selves) and now transformed into hunters, initiands are able to inject a new vitality – "rebounding violence" – into the community of

---

[13] See Kitts (2017b) for some ancient Near Eastern representations.

hunter-adults, who may harness that revitalization in triumphalist aggression toward exterior threats (Bloch 1992:24–37).

According to Bloch, similar overcoming is discernible among the Dinka, whose culture is built around cattle. A keen identification of individuals with cattle is exploited in healing rituals, wherein the victim of illness is urged to submit to his illness and then to sacrifice a bovine (vicariously the ill part of himself), whose vitality is perceived as vanquished, as illness, by the individual's own acts of speech. The speech is perceived as invoking an unchanging and conquering power superior to the power of cattle, and both the conquering and cattle-like powers are seen as penetrating one's human self. According to Bloch, the sacrificial process is acutely distressing because of the great attachment of the Dinka to their cattle. This peculiar opposition of cattle vitality (which absorbs illness) and vital speech (powerful enough to drain the animal of vitality) is deeply felt when, for instance, the beloved animal becomes twitching flesh at the moment of killing and the human voice becomes possessed by a divine voice.[14]

Bloch (1992) sees similar processes of vicarious immersion into dying or nearly dying victims and then the socioreligious vanquishing of them as played out in biblical and Greek myths. This extension of his theory is surely an overreach (though Greek and biblical myths do bring their own kinds of trauma to bear), but Bloch's connection of trauma with the creation of culture is nonetheless intriguing. His core hypothesis is that group cohesion and aggression are rooted in an emotional trauma induced by the specter of violence for the individual members.

Physical as well as emotional trauma is explored by Harvey Whitehouse in terms of the imagistic mode of religious experience and the changes it induces for individuals and groups. The imagistic mode – more personally transformative than the doctrinal, repetitive mode – is triggered by rare performances of highly

---

[14] Bloch (1992) references Lienhardt (1961:137) on this spirit possession.

arousing, cognitively shocking rituals rooted in pageantry and, for our purposes here, in painful ordeal, as seen in an array of groups from traditional warrior cults to paramilitary cells (2004:124). Head-biting, evulsion of fingernails, whipping, burning, mutilation, extreme physical deprivation, and agonizing circumcisions are some of these worldwide "rites of terror" (Whitehouse 2004:111), the painful and traumatic nature of which demands reflection on the neurological, socio-logical, and other changes elicited by such ordeals. Whitehouse's cognitive theory of the imagistic religious mode integrates three elements: flash-bulb memory, neurological changes, and the spontaneous exegetical reflection triggered by trauma.

The first, flash-bulb memory, is episodic memory characterized by the retrieval of fine-grained background information with a vivid focus on con-textual details, extending into visual and tactile impressions not directly rele-vant to the sequence of traumatic events (Whitehouse 2004:106). Flash-bulb memory is a well-known element in post-traumatic stress disorder, wherein memories tend to be difficult to fully suppress and may erupt into consciousness for years after the traumatic event.

The second element, neurological change associated with heightened perceptions during trauma, has been explained in a variety of ways: as localized neurological damage; as high brain glucose arousal in experiences of stress; as implicating different subcortical circuits pending episodic, procedural, and semantic memories, etc. (Whitehouse 2004:106). Generally, it is accepted that specific properties of neural functioning are excited by trauma and probably involve limbic and reticular systems and diffuse emissions across the cortex (Whitehouse 2004:107); obviously, such changes will be profound.

The third element, spontaneous exegetical reflection, is seen as a psychological response to traumatic ordeal, entailing initially a frantic search for meaning (where there may be no precedent), followed by a process of analogical reasoning (Whitehouse 2004:113) which draws on symbolic and thematic associations from one's experience. These reflections may not gel into semantic and transmissible knowledge for decades. When they do so gel, they may be grasped as revelatory knowledge elusive to simple verbal transmission. Hence, fully fledged members of imagistically based groups ensure that new initiands undergo similar processes of traumatic ordeal, which inspire for initiands similar exegetical reflections based in iconic or symbolic associations.

These three features of the imagistic mode of religious experience not only result in traumatic changes for individuals; there are also social ramifications. Rites of terror, as Whitehouse calls them, may startle, transform, and cement initiands into exclusive, impregnable communities who may experience powerful motivations to perpetuate trauma, not just on new initiands but outward onto other groups, occasionally in terroristic forms (Whitehouse 2004:119–136).

Alcorta and Sosis similarly ponder the roles of pain and violence in personal and social transformations, but their approach is based on costly signaling theory, the neurological realities of adolescence, and the evolution of religion. Specifically, they attempt to explain the evolutionary advantage of painful rites of passage, which are too common worldwide to be attributed to cultural idiosyncrasy. Such ordeals may involve kidnapping, isolation, food and sleep deprivation, scarification, genital mutilation, physical torture, exposure to hideous demons and gods and stories about them, and other shocking traumas (2013:571–596) which seem to put adolescents at risk. To probe the possible adaptive benefit for a society who would so put its adolescents at risk, Alcorta and Sosis consider adolescent brains which, being in the midst of profound changes in the dopominergic and synaptic systems, are particularly receptive to stimuli and are primed for the effects of trauma.[15] The effects may be delineated into three (so

---

[15] "During adolescence, the reward value of inherently pleasurable stimuli, such as food, sex, drugs, and music, peaks and the brain's dopaminergic systems undergo substantial reorganization. At the same time, the prefrontal cortex and the temporal

delineated by the present author), which interrelate. The first two effects address individual changes, and the third group behavior.

First, violent and painful experiences "construct" individual personalities. That is, they stimulate the senses, induce autonomic changes in adolescents' brains, and evoke intense emotions which may be suppressed but are nearly impossible to erase.[16] Such effects endure in personal histories and shape identities.

Second, violent and painful experiences may be argued to construct social and religious realities. Such experiences invest cultural symbols, beliefs, and other abstractions with emotional significance, so that the adolescents become attached to them. Others have noticed the reifying consequence of pain. Beidelman observed during fieldwork that painful experience actually may confer a quality of incontestable reality on the source that brings the pain into being (1997:179), and Glucklich pointed out that "strong feelings induced

cortex mature. The prefrontal cortex is the brain region responsible for impulse inhibition, social judgment, personal decision making, and abstract reasoning; the temporal cortex functions in face recognition, music, language, and the integration of other social stimuli. . . . This synaptic reorganization in social and executive processing regions of the brain occurs in tandem with heightened adolescent reward salience and emotional responsivity. These changes in the structures and circuitry of the adolescent brain provide a unique developmental window for linking social experiences with abstract, symbolic representations and investing those representations with emotional significance and reward value capable of influencing subsequent social judgments and behavioral choices. Religious ritual appears to be optimally designed to do just that" (Alcorta and Sosis 2013:582–583 [internal citations omitted]).

[16] "[T]the conditioned association of sacred symbols with violently evoked negative emotions and painful body states through terror, violence, and sacred pain is motivationally powerful and nearly impossible to extinguish" (Alorta and Sosis 2013:581).

by pain affect our capacity to perceive and know reality" (2003:150). Strikingly, Alcorta and Sosis assert that the more counterintuitive and supernatural the religious abstractions attached to painful experience, the more likely they are to arrest attention and impress themselves into adolescent mentalities.

Third, from an evolutionary perspective, the advantage of painful cuttings and other traumatic ordeals is that, while fomenting shared trauma, they cement individuals together in a way that may mobilize the group against outsiders. As do Bloch and Whitehouse, Alcorta and Sosis (2013) note the bonding that occurs among adolescents who undergo painful and violent rites of passage together. One adaptive benefit of such ordeals is precisely cooperative, especially among groups for whom hunting and war are prevalent activities and among groups which have become too large to guarantee the necessary social cohesion for such activities: "Participation in such rituals promotes ingroup cooperation through the neurophysiological mechanisms previously discussed, and it also signals group commitment to others" so that cultural "freeloaders" drop out (Alcorta and Sosis 2013:586). In other terms, the shared experiences of pain fortify and rarefy group solidarity.

Ultimately, defining religion as primarily a socializing phenomenon (in a Durkheimian sense) and seeking to understand its evolutionary function in human survival, Alcorta and Sosis see the violence imposed on adolescents as more than a component of religion. The pain imposed by violence actually may be an evolutionary catalyst for religion (2013:589), based on the capacity of violently induced pain to construct individual personalities and social realities, and to generate experiences of social unity.[17]

Whether or not these three anthropological theories may be taken as universally apt, a striking point in all three is that experiences of pain, violence,

---

[17] See also Alan Morinis on the mutilation of the body as a potent symbolization of the socialization of the self (1985).

and trauma are held to resonate more deeply in personal development and social relations than are experiences of pleasure and joy. As Rappaport put it in 1999, there is something perlocutionary about pain (1999:147). All three theories further imply that painful and traumatic experiences bring about personal and social transformations while eluding discursive formulations by the experiencers. Notably, their effects are often interpreted in terms of religion.

Religious Violence as Performance Violence

"Rebounding violence" and "rites of terror" resonate with the social impact of large-scale destructive events which are often linked with religion. Regarding the aforementioned prediscursive element, religious scholars and anthropologists now forage increasingly through the semantic fields of the poetic, the artistic, or even the ontological for new ways to describe shifts in public perspective subsequent to acts of global terror (Strathern and Stewart 2006, Crapanzano 2004, Schmidt and Schröder 2001, Aijmer and Abbink 2000). We hear of an emerging sense of the uncanny, of bodily (virtual) contingency, of social unpredictability and of the "potential rupture within our customary worlds" (Strathern and Stewart 2006:7). Corresponding to the ever-more permeable boundaries of those customary worlds are our ever-more conflicted responses, as we see in our entanglement in wars and in rumors of wars, as well as in some very public acts of domestic terror too numerous to list. The staged aspects to those acts of terror with proclaimed religious foundations are difficult to ignore. Performance violence is a relatively new rubric for understanding the violence associated with religion and borrows explicitly from the semantic field of theater. Jeffrey Alexander's dramaturgical analysis and also Bernhard Giesen's description of primary, secondary, and tertiary ritual performances, which are implicitly theatrical,[18] are touched upon later. Here

---

[18] See, for instance, Juergensmeyer and Kitts (2011) and Juergensmeyer, Kitts, and Jerryson (2013).

the focus is on three well-established theories of religious violence associated with the rubric of performance: those of Mark Juergensmeyer, René Girard, and Walter Burkert.

Juergensmeyer's contribution is notable because it is derived from interviews with activists charged with acts of terrorism. In this sense it is based on contemporary field data rather than sheer conjecture, and takes the insider's point of view as bearing on the *epistēmē*, as Foucault called it, on which social actors rely – even if this *epistēmē* includes inarticulate elements (per Foucault). Taking the insider's view seriously is explained by the sociotheological approach to religious violence (Juergensmeyer and Sheikh 2013). The sociotheological approach dismisses the tendency to analyze religiously based terrorism in terms of a secular–religious divide (a bifurcated thinking habit traceable to the Enlightenment) and sees rational choice theory and strategic analyses as dully incommensurate with acts of suicide terrorism and with the immaterial, long-term rewards that those activists say they expect. Instead, it embraces religious language and aspirations as offering distinctive lenses into the social and metaphysical realities perceived by some violent actors (Juergensmeyer and Sheikh 2013). Those realities, as outlined by Juergensmeyer in numerous publications (e.g., 2000, 2013), adduce cosmic significance to extraordinary acts of destruction; hence his coinage, "cosmic war." Spectacularly staged, conducted in a ritualized way, and vested in inducing witnesses to imagine the event through the designer's eyes, the terrorist's performance violence is comparable to street theater: it confronts spectators with an alternative view of reality and entices spectators to embrace it, if only for a moment. Not all violent performances are religiously based, of course, but violent performances invoking religious scriptures and religious hopes often implicate supernatural agencies, Armageddon-like expectations, and, perhaps ironically, visions of ultimate world peace. Participants in a cosmic war may conduct violent acts with a stark urgency incomprehensible to outsiders: hence the astonishing scale of the performance violence associated with religious terrorism. Acts of cosmic war are designed seemingly to startle witnesses into a new level of not only sociological but ontological insecurity.

The notion of performance violence is also central to the scapegoating theory associated with René Girard. Girard saw socially staged spectacles of violence – e.g., public executions, dramatized simulations of martyrs' deaths, animal sacrifices – as defusing a more lethal, chaotic, and uncontrollable violence which otherwise would beset and destroy societies. The theory, derived from an eclectic mix of literary narratives and anthropological field reports, is based on mimetic rivalry, a sociopsychological disposition which he saw as inexorable in human groups. According to Girard, our tendency to perpetuate both symbolic and actual in our rituals and institutions arises ultimately from a deep-seated anxiety about our intrinsic self-worth ("being," as he called it [1977:146]). Subject to this self-doubt, individuals suspect that their "rivals" have more of this being, and so imitate them, which threatens them and leads to potentially endless cycles of reciprocal violence and vendetta (Girard 2014a:5, 37; 1987:26; 2014b:13–14). It is because we have no internal braking system on this mimetic tendency (a presumption of the theory [Mack 1987:8]) that societies have felt compelled to develop ploys to eliminate the potential violence between rivals before it breaks out. Those ploys may be formalized as religious sacrifices, as exhibitions of collective retribution (e.g., stonings, hangings, mock-battles), or as any number of violent spectacles which rely on collectively acceptable aetiologies. Regardless of their public rationales, the deeper sociopsychological purpose of such staged spectacles, according to Girard, is to redirect the violence naturally arising among rivals onto substitutes, or scapegoats, chosen for their similarities to actual rivals, but also for their peripheral value in society.[19] These scapegoats may die in public

---

[19] See Girard (1987:27; 2014b:2, 21).

and often gruesome ways, or be remembered as doing so. By so dying they absorb vicariously the mimetic rivalry and reciprocal violence which otherwise would implode into acts of "unanimous violence" and destroy the social order. Their deaths, replayed in myths and rituals, rivet attention and divert impulses for mimetic rivalry. Thus, scapegoats function as saviors, which is how they may be remembered in myth and cult.

Girard's central tenet – that violence fascinates us because of its implicit anarchy and threat to our personal and social safety – is not new. Violence as a rivet for cultural imagination has fascinated scholars of religion, who cannot help but notice that narratives of primordial violence lie at the heart of many religious traditions. But that rivet has drawn comment from scholars in other fields too. In *Totem and Taboo* (1946 [1918]), Freud described violently themed rituals as defusing potential social violence into the guilty worship of an order-maintaining father figure. In *Myth and Cult among Primitive Peoples* (1963), Jensen saw a soteriological impulse in Indonesian rituals commemorating the murderous death of legume-bearing Hainuwele. Indeed, the soteriological implications of ritualized violence have been recognized since Robertson-Smith. These grand theories of religious violence have drawn considerable attention, but also sharp criticism by experts in particular traditions, including by myself.[20] Still, given the panorama of religious legends implicating some kind of core human violence, it is difficult simply to dismiss the urge toward grand theories to explain our fascination with the theme. Of these grand theories, Walter Burkert's was perhaps the most significant twentieth century contribution.

On the subject of performance violence, Walter Burkert took the long view in nearly all of his writings, most of which address early evidence for religion and ritual. In his famous *Homo Necans* (1983), he traced the evolutionary roots of ancient Greek and Near Eastern staged killings of domesticated

---

[20] Kitts (2002, 2016).

animals back to the prehistoric "hunting apes," our earliest meat-eating ances-tors (recently identified by him as *Homo Erectus* [Burkert 2013]). Faced with the slow and bloody deaths of their fellow mammals – human-like in so many features – and yet aspiring to eat meat, early predatorial bands of humans, said Burkert, experienced alternating emotions of horror and elation, compassion and excitement, regret and thrill. This emotional ambivalence bonded the group together, but, more importantly, indelibly imprinted our collective mental development as a genus, particularly since the emergence of *Homo Sapiens Sapiens* – a great practitioner of ritual. As Burkert saw it, over millennia these polar emotions of horror and elation became fused and perpetuated in the religious practice of sacrifice, wherein domesticated animals were led to auspi-cious and ritualized deaths. In Homer's Odyssey and in Greek tragedy, human discomfort with this staged killing is betrayed by layers of deceit: the sacrificial knife initially is hidden in a basket of grains, the animal is made to gesture a mock-consent, and the screams of women stir the crowd, lead to the climax of cutting the animal's throat, and also drown out the bellowing and death rattle of the dying victim (Burkert 1983:5).[21] At the same time, these sacrificial specta-cles were occasions for the jubilant eating of meat. We are the only carnivore to make a ceremony out of killing and eating meat, and, in ancient times, the only one to require a holy sanction for it in the form of offering animal meat on a sacred altar (Burkert 2013:440–442). Ancient piety was tantamount to a willingness to conduct this sacred slaughter, often as a state obligation. That this office transcended the need for food is conspicuous in the occasional human sacrifice, or legend thereof, to which no immediate dietary benefit seemingly would accrue (Burkert 2013:443).

---

[21] In the Iliad, the animal victim's death is never acknowledged in commensal sacrifice (unlike in oath-sacrifice), but rather the whole ritual is couched in terms of cuisine (Kitts 2011, 2012, 2015).

Regardless of how the practice of sacrifice emerged, it remains a startling fact that, as Burkert saw it, early literary records make ritualized killing the basic experience of the "sacred" and religion's most prominent feature. For Burkert, the same feature is perpetuated today in the guise of sacrificial symbolizations and, less directly, in the exhortations to wars, both internal and external, proclaimed from religious pulpits. Taking the long view, Burkert (2013) argued that religion, and more particularly the performance of religious sacrifice, accomplished two functions for our species and for ours alone: First, it engaged us with a seemingly natural struggle for existence by staging a confrontation of life and death on its altars, and brought that struggle to the fore of human consciousness. Second, it displaced anxieties about that confrontation by creating a superworld of deities and rationales that sanctioned the serious business of killing and eating meat (2013:450). Thus, "[r]eligion acknowledges danger, fear, and violence, while presenting rules concerning how to deal with them, one of which [addresses] the risk and the triumph of killing" (2013:450).

All three of these well-known theories make violence a magnet for religious imagination, and two of them are established purportedly in ancient evidence. But is ancient evidence proof for a universal predisposition for violence? What evidence do we need to support theories about a human disposition for or against violence? Although the ancient evidence cannot be conclusive, it is pointless to avoid the question of this reputedly innate tendency, a question which has been pursued by war historians, archaeologists, anthropologists, and even paleontologists.

Staged Violence in the Longest View

Interpretive Problems

The theme of violence and its impact has preoccupied audiences at least since our ancient Near Eastern epics, hymns, treaties, and cursing texts, some traceable to at least the third millennium BCE or even earlier (Kitts 2013, 2017b). Many of those representations of violence are bound up with religion. Not only do we find prayers and poems exalting gods of the storm and gods who march in battles, but also curses promising divine vengeance on treaty-breakers, battle boasts of piling up heads and reddening rivers with blood, and reports of divine retribution and battlefield favor (gods "running in front"). To top it off, we have artistic spectacles and ritual reports which seem to exalt the power to kill (Bahrani 2003, 2004, 2008; Collon 2003; Noegel 2007; Olyan 2014, 2016), and archaeological hints of ritualized killing at burials, altars, boundaries, and building foundations (Green 2003; Schwemer 2007, 2008; Weinfeld 1990; Archi 1975). Controversy surrounds the evidence, however. Some ancient war and threat texts are clearly propagandistic (Holloway 2002; Noegel 2007). Many derive from the era of early city-states, for whom competitive interests might have been served by displays of strong force – not only military force, but force as inferred through proclamation, poetry, iconography, and ritual. As for human sacrificial death, we are warned by historians of antiquity that archaeological evidence for sacrificial death rarely is cleanly distinguishable from evidence for any other kind of violent death (Ferguson 2008; Hughes 1991), except when human remains are associated with other material evidence, such as altars, foundation stones, or royal burials. To complicate matters, textual evidence and archaeological evidence are known to disagree. The Bible reports child sacrifice and passing children through fire (e.g., 2 Kings 23:10; Is. 57, Ez. 20:27–31, Jer. 30), but the propagandistic nature of these reports casts a shadow over their reliability, and the material evidence for child sacrifice, say at Carthage, is hotly contested (Niditch 1993, Levinson 1993; Xella 2013). Such interpretive difficulties require us to extend our focus beyond the ancient Near East to preliterate societies as traceable in the anthropological, archaeological, and paleontological record.

Most anthropological studies of a human predisposition for or against violence, particularly in the forms of war and feuding, seek out extant simple societies – usually acephalous and unsegmented societies – as models for the most ancient, in order to derive universalizing schemata about cross-cultural patterns based on common sociologies and ecologies. But critics challenge the presumption that extant simple societies provide accurate mirrors for the social processes of prehistoric societies. They ask, for instance, how would we recognize the accuracy of such a mirror in the first place? What are we to deduce from the fact that contemporary ethnographic data and ancient archaeological data often do not match (Kelly 2000:2; Ferguson 1997:424–425, 2006:470–474), even where ecologies seem to? Some point out that data drawn from today's simple societies, or even primate societies, cannot possibly be pristine, since those societies already are disturbed by Western ethnographers in their quest for evidence (Whitehead 2007; Ferguson 2006). Critics also target the skewing of evidence based on showcasing violence in the first place: a one-pointed focus blinds us to other factors, they claim, such as how or if violence is even perceived as such.[22] Regarding the theories of Girard and Burkert, some scholars dismiss the likelihood of an "ontic seizure" at the heart of social imagination everywhere, preferring to examine instead individual societies, their "exegetical ingenuity," their "imagination and intellection of culture" and their concepts of process and work (J. Z. Smith 2004:148–150). Yet other theorists tie different degrees of sedentism in relatively simple societies – e.g., hunter-gatherers who store food, or pastoral groups who seasonally practice agriculture – with proneness for conflict based on resource-accumulation and competition. But we must acknowledge, with Knauft, that the variation in support for conflict among extant resource-accumulating prestate societies is enormous (1991:393–394). All this

---

[22] This argument is self-evident, but see discussion of the Kamajors, above, as an illustration.

makes it difficult to assume primordial patterns based on contemporary parallels. In short, problems abound.

On the matter of an inherent human propensity to war, scholars disagree, of course. Margaret Meade challenged the premise decades ago, noting that highly conventionalized displays of violence, as in warfare, may be treated as human inventions like any other – marriage, alphabets and syllabaries, slavery, trial by ordeal, or jury systems. She traced the process by which these arise in culture and history, not in human biology (Meade 1940). Like Knauft, she also pointed out that extant simple societies were not all the same. In her view, some Alaskan hunter-gatherers may have accepted displays of individualized violence – e.g., fights and killings over wives – but did not practice group warfare, whereas hunter-gatherers elsewhere, such as the Sioux or Maori, may have regarded war as a prestige game and sought to excel at it. The fighting we call war, therefore, is not tied to one natural setting or social structure.

The most vociferous opponent to this historical-cultural point of view is probably Lawrence Keeley, who argues that war is endemic to 90–95 percent of societies (1996:28), simple and complex, throughout the archaeological and historical record. Keeley notes numerous examples of individualized traumatic death in the evidence for preliterate societies from Europe, North Africa, and the Americas (1996:36–39), and accuses anthropologists who deny primordial bellicosity of Rousseauian blinders. He does acknowledge that societies endowed with simple weapons may practice war on a less deadly scale and terminate it earlier, but claims also that they stage battles more frequently than modern societies (1996:42–48), and so are not inherently less lethal. It is sometimes argued that violent ritual, sport, or cultural display might assuage urges to violence in simple societies (e.g., Nash 2005:80),[23] to which Keeley responds

---

[23] E.g., see discussion of the potlatch as symbolic warfare among the Kwakiutl and Hagen, in Stewart and Strathern (2014, chapter 3).

that such strategies are limited in effect and successful only when adversaries are related or share conventional practices and understandings (1996:59–67). In response to the claim that the presence of Western ethnographers might significantly amplify the bellicosity of extant simple societies (e.g., the claims of Whitehead (2007) and Ferguson (2006, 2008), mentioned earlier), Keeley strongly denies it, reasoning that the exposure of simple societies to modernity would not differ essentially from the exposure of simple societies historically to any other culture in terms of introducing novel weapons, customs, disease, resource competition, ideological clashes, etc. (1996:28). But critics point out that Keeley ignores the scale of Western impact and its potential to intensify perceptions of conflicting realities (cf. Ferguson 2006:476–479). His fiercest critics see Keeley's argument as challenged by its Hobbesian versus Rousseauian polarities and by his discounting of whole swathes of archaeological data where there is no sign of violence. This last omission would seem fatal to his argument (Ferguson 2006:480–497, 1997:425; Thorpe 2003:153–154).

Generally speaking, anthropologists agree that individualized acts of homicide occur in most if not all human societies (Fuentes 2004:715; Kelly 2000); it is the ubiquity of organized warfare, inter-group feuding, and related cultural developments that is disputed. Evolutionary anthropologists, such as Fuentes, see the notion of primordial bellicosity as simple, at best (2004, 2009), as do Knauft, et al., who hold up displays of aggression and male dominance by other primates to our own behaviors (1991). Ours are considerably less muscular. They see the success of our species over the long term as due not to the forceful elimination of rival groups through collective violence and not due to the inadvertent elimination of rivals through the success of mating and resource gathering strategies and subsequent DNA inheritances. Rather, they see our fitness for success as due instead to our creative forms of affiliation, cooperation, and competition in response to a multitude of factors, but especially to change (Fuentes 2004, 2009; Visala and Fuentes 2015; Knauft, et al. 1991). We are the most adaptable and migratory of creatures. Neither the Hobbesian notion of innate human aggression nor the Rousseauian view of our Eden-like beginnings acknowledges our behavioral adaptability and complex mobility over the last 200,000 years (as *Homo Sapiens Sapiens*), not to mention the adaptability and mobility of hominids over the last 2.5 million.

Another problem with the claim of primordial human bellicosity is an unstated assumption that the last 500 years of human history reflect a pattern for all of humanity for all time. Material evidence from the last 500 years shows far more violence than does the evidence for any period before this (Ferguson 2008:27), an increase which, admittedly, could be due to many factors: population growth, resource competition, innovations and expansions in warring technologies, etc. But as Ferguson sees it, although collective violence did not emerge out of thin air in the last 500 years, its universality among all populations everywhere cannot be proved by reference to this material evidence, either.

Archaeological Considerations

Notwithstanding the interpretive problems, archaeologists see the historical debate as pivoting ultimately on material evidence – namely, on the signs of the entry of warfare into the archaeological record (Arkush and Allen 2006:2–4). Some, with Keeley, contend that warfare is as old or older than fully modern humans, while others contend that it arose with the transition to sedentism, or with the advent of the first states.

Unfortunately, spotty data from presedentary societies weakens either kind of contention. For instance, the earliest roving bands built no fortifications and used no specialized weapons that we can tie narrowly to intra-societal aggression. When we do get fortifications, burned settlements, and what appear to be weapons, there is the problem of discerning purpose. Fortification walls, at least as old as eighth millennium BCE Jericho, may be built to keep in stock and keep out predators, rather than to thwart invaders (Keyes Roper 1969:429), or conceivably for both purposes. Burned settlements might be the result of accident rather than attack. Prehistoric bows and arrows, spears, even maces might serve hunting rather than war. Axes and scythes may serve agriculture rather than fighting, or possibly may serve both. It is not until the Neolithic era that we find decorated weapons in burials, signifying the probable existence of a warrior elite (Ferguson 2008). Once our ancestors invent bronze and iron, tools/weapons become harder, and the evidence for violence becomes more profuse – although ancient war historians warn us repeatedly against simple technological determinism (e.g., Escheverría Rey 2010). For earlier periods, we lack clear evidence of the way tools were used, and thus for the interpersonal violence to which such tools may have been applied (Thorpe 2003:150).

Skeletal evidence is slightly more supportive of interpersonal violence than is weaponry. Cranial depressions consistent with bludgeoning go all the way back to 780,000 BCE (Ferguson 2008:15–16), or conceivably as far back as Australopithecines some four million years ago (Keyes Roper 1969:432–33)! But the early evidence relevant to the collective violence of fully modern humans derives mostly from the Upper Paleolithic period, particularly in Europe, where research has a long history. The evidence includes caches of skeletal bones (e.g., a 7,000-year-old bone deposit at Talheim, Germany, and a 7,500-year-old "skull nest" in Bavarian Ofnet [Ferguson 2008:18]) and skulls pierced with embedded points (Ferguson 2008:15). Here again, discerning cause is not straightforward. In themselves, damaged or altered human skulls may be due to falling boulders, hunting accidents, predeath fighting matches (e.g., wrestling contests), the ritualized head-banging known to be a component of Australian grieving rituals, preburial defleshing (as in sky burials), skull plastering (as at Jericho and Çatal Höyük) – or must they all be due to war? As Thorpe summarizes, caches of human bones might be an outcome of violent attack, but might equally be an outcome of disease or starvation (2003:152). Caches of skulls might be war trophies, but might also reflect ritualized corpse treatments or cannibalism. In cranial depressions one scholar may see the cannibalism of brains while another might suppose a skull cult (Keyes Roper 1969:430).[24] It should be noted that historically known cannibals rarely eat humans for nutrition, but rather for other reasons, such as reverence for the dead, spite for the enemy, as a deliberate strategy for power-deprivation by captors who seek to thwart competitors' ingestion of a fellow-warrior's power (Thorpe 2003:158), or as a threatening display. The upshot is that purely statistical data for skeletal evidence, whether broken bones or depressed or cached skulls, cannot prove significance, and context is always debatable.

An implicit element in this discussion is ideology, which of course is difficult to discern in the archaeological record. In extant simple societies ideology is crucial to whether or not there is a "culture of war" (Arkush and Allen 2006:3–4), consisting of, for instance, a propensity to train youths to engage in martial activities, to seek vengeance, or to resolve disputes by fighting. Personal honor tends to be very important in extant small societies where everyone knows each other and clan identities define individuals, as among the Yanomami of the Amazon, who are studied precisely for their propensity to violence (Thorpe 2003:160; Chagnon 1988). Also relevant to a discussion of primordial warring is the notion of social substitutability, wherein one member of a group may become a target for the perceived misdeeds of another. Whereas crimes of individual passion occur in all human groups, not all societies allow or condone making targets for reprisal the friends, family, or group members of an offender who has committed an

---

[24] Bashed skulls are relatively frequent in the record (Keyes Roper 1969:442–448), especially among Neanderthals (Keeley 1996:37), who hunted with spears. See also Thorpe 2003:151.

initial harm (Kelly 2000, Fuentes 2004). Nor do all groups take it upon the collective to seek retribution on behalf of an individual. Group identity in the form of collective guilt and collective vengeance, according to Kelly, is a concomitant of the social logic of feuding, not to mention of outright war. But lacking some kind of identity marker in human remains (some kind of corporeal modification, for instance), how might we detect this kind of felt collectivity in the deep archaeological record? Finally, war-magic, as attested among the Yanomami and New Guinean Avitap (Thorpe 2003:148), rarely leaves an archaeological trace; yet, as inferred in the earlier discussion of the Kamajors, it can be quite relevant to bravery and menace in battle. In sum, evidence of ideology of any kind is difficult to trace in the ancient material record and what evidence there may be is difficult to elucidate contextually.

Some scholars claim to see warring ideology in prehistoric art. Yet our few artistic representations of apparent conflict for preliterate people are notoriously difficult to interpret. Ferguson provides the example of a Bronze Age carving at Fossum in Bohuslän, Sweden, which depicts two match-stick-like men standing on a boat and wielding battle axes, but not striking with them (2008:19). On the surface the carving appears to represent an imminent fight, but other art from that Bronze Age culture features match-stick-like boats and individuals holding battle axes in the ready position when there is no opponent in sight (see Bahn 1998:55, 68, 183, 199, 210). Hence, there are stylistic questions. Given this artistic pattern and the lack of wounding scenes, the carving at Bohuslän might equally represent not a battle but a clan insignia, as Ferguson points out, or some kind of ritual performance (2008:19, as also suggested by Nash 2005:80). Symbolic violence is of course a well-known feature of many smaller societies – and sometimes, according to Nash, the least damaging vehicle for releasing social stresses (2005:80). Nash conjectures a ritual purpose, conceivably a dance, for the Spanish Neolithic Levantine rock-representations from the Gasulla and Valltorta gorges. These paintings show warriors running at each other and wielding bows, but no dead or pierced warriors (2005:82). Elsewhere in the Levantine art, though (at Cingle de la Mola Remigia), there is an apparent victim, represented with six arrows protruding from his slumped body. On another panel is a possible display of camaraderie wherein a slain warrior is carried in the arms of another (Nash 2005:82). Although it is dangerous to attribute particular meanings to such very ancient art, at least this latter image would appear to suggest some kind of narrative emotionality. Unlike the famous Upper Paleolithic art from France and Italy, these Spanish representations depict human rather than animal forms. Presumably some kind of ideology is involved, although it is difficult to identify it.

Of the well-known Upper Paleolithic rock or cave wall art of Western Europe,[25] there are no illustrations of human-on-human violence (Bahn 1998:196–197), with two conceivable exceptions. Those are the two apparently speared human torsos painted amidst moving animals on the cave wall at Grotte de Cougnac. Unless the artists conflated human meat with animal meat, the speared human torsos complicate the popular dreaming-the-hunt hypothesis associated with these murals since Henri Brueil (discussed by Bahn 1998:62–63). Could the human figures at Cougnac signal a felt resemblance between hunted animals and humans? The visages of the painted and engraved animals in the caves at Cougnac and Chauvet are certainly sympathetic enough,[26] but the human figures at Cougnac have no faces at all, or, in one case, a seeming animal face, if not body.

---

[25] The ancient art from 40,000 to 10,000 years ago (the era we consider upper Paleolithic) is not just European, of course. We do have Australian rock art of the same general age (Bar-Yosef 2002:368).

[26] For a summary of theories of visual pleasure at perceiving forms homologous to the human face and body, see Glucklich (2003:63–65) and Bryan Turner (1992:107–112).

As a point of comparison, others ponder the rock art not as wishful hunting fantasies, but as indicating trance and out-of-body experiences (as among the San of South Africa [see Conkey 1987; Bahn 1998:240–242]), ancestral or supernatural figures (particularly for the therianthropes, described by Bahn at 1998:230–232), sorcery, shamanism, and dream representations (Bahn 1998:233; 235–239). It is simply impossible to know what purpose, if any, was intended by the artists who made these, or if they even considered this art. There is a rich literature debating the significance of these cultural products, which date back conceivably to Homo Erectus![27] The extent to which these ancient cultural products support violent practices, or even the notion of violence, is contestable.

The long and short of it is that violence is a subject of acute interest for moderns, and evidence of prehistoric interest in it remains conjectural.

Section II: Ritual

Like the study of violence, the study of ritual has ongoing relevance to human behavior, given that we participate in rituals today and have done so, according to inscribed evidence, at least since the Near Eastern Bronze Age, and likely very much earlier.[28] Yet scholarly inquiries about the topic are only about a century old and questions remain basic: What are rituals? Why do we perform them? Are ritual actors doing what they say they are doing, or is there some other motive, which eludes intention? How may we

---

[27] See review by Chippindale (1999).

[28] On organized dance represented on seals and pottery in the ancient Near East from as early as the sixth millennium BCE, see Collon (2003). On evolutionary issues, ethologists remind us that we are hardly the only species to engage in ritual behavior and that our rituals share features with those of animals. See, e.g., Dissanayake (1979).

distinguish ritualized behavior from nonritualized? What are ritual's social effects? What are its personal effects? Are there particular social or personal circumstances which rituals tend to serve? How do our rituals compare to those of other species? Why do some rituals have more transformative effects on participants than others? And so on. Typical rubrics have ranged from the dramatizations of myth, rites of passage, efforts at worldly transcendence, sacralizations of power, evolutionary survivals, species' signaling behavior, neurotic habits, play, socialization, metaphorical transformation, special framing of experience, and liturgical orders, to reflections of doctrinal and imagistic modes of religious experience. With proffered answers come thorny complications. This part of the book introduces some basic theories about the nature of ritual insofar as these theories may help us to ponder ritual's potential relationship with violence. As in Section I, illustrations pepper the text.

As pointed out in the introduction, good arguments may be made that ritual experience eludes discursive dissection altogether. Indeed, whole volumes are dedicated to this discursive elusiveness and intrinsic problems with theorizing rituals,[29] since ritual theories frequently end up less meaty than actual ritual experience. One disputed issue is meaning. Some scholars scorn attempts to impute any meaning to the formalized behavior we call rituals, while others argue that a ritual form, or frame, never comes to us quite empty and that in fact the frame itself communicates something, although that something may actually shift over time, despite traditional attempts to preserve it.[30] Arguments are intricate.

[29] E.g., Handelman and Lindquist, eds., 2004, and Stausberg, Snoek, Kreinath, eds., 2006.

[30] For a cogent summary of arguments for ritual's meaningfulness and meaninglessness, see Michaels (2006: 247–261).

An introductory volume seeking to grasp violent intent and violent expression in ritual must grapple precisely with meaning – or, more descriptively, with ideation. Ideation and form, or substance and form, thought and action, belief and rite, picture and frame, meaning and event, *Geist* and *Natur*, and similar dichotomies long have beset ritual theory (Rappaport 1999; Bell 1992:16ff, Stewart and Strathern 2014; Ricoeur 1973:99–100, 104). However intellectualist, such bifurcations are strategic at first blush because they highlight the issue of intended meaning in ritual, while pointing to the aforementioned problem of discerning such meanings by discursive analysis alone. It is pointless to avoid the issue of meaning in pondering violent rituals, if only to take seriously the claimed intentions of ritual participants. Here, in order to focus on the experience of the ritual participant, rather than on the broader meaningfulness of the human phenomenon of ritual – its evolutionary purpose, for instance – we will cast the current discussion in terms of ideas, or more precisely of ideation, rather than of meaning.

By "ideation" is meant the emergence of ideas, images, and awareness, including sensory-affective awareness and a sense of personal transformation and social identity, for ritual practitioners or their witnesses, or both. By formalization is meant embodied behavior, encompassing rhythm, kinesthetics, sequential fixity or elasticity, expressive register, alterations in temporal modalities and group dynamics, etc. Ideation and formalization obviously intertwine, but for schematic purposes will be unpacked separately in the following sections.

Ritual Ideation

When does the purported idea for the ritual bear on its performance – at the ritual's inception, its result, or somewhere inbetween?[31] For instance, considering violence

[31] Most theorists do subscribe to the notion that ritual may be seen minimally as organized behavior which is less technical than symbolic in outcome (Handelman

as typically understood, one might distinguish between the imagination which impels the performance of, say, a blood-sacrifice, oath for vengeance, or mystical assault, from the awareness which emerges as a result of it, maybe awe, respect for authority, commitment to a goal, or, more ominously, horror, hate, and menacing mood. Such an awareness might be deemed a ritual artifact, culturally produced, whereas the impelling motivations imply, minimally, an exercise in instrumental logic. Where do these intersect, if they do, and how do they bear on ritual experience?

Some Traditional Approaches

In one form or another, the issue of ideation has exercised theoretical minds since at least William Robertson-Smith, who at the end of the nineteenth century discounted it, seeing ideation as a mere accretion upon collective practice. Specifically, myth and creed were secondary to ritual practice and "merely part of the apparatus of the worship; they served to excite the fancy and sustain the interest of the worshipper; but he was offered a choice of several accounts . . . no one cared what he believed about its origin" (1998 [1889]:28). The secondary character of myth was to be explained as the product of nascent philosophizing or as a political mechanism designed to unify the various worshipping behaviors of originally distinct social groups (1998 [1889]:29). His example was biblical sacrifice which, he said, preceded its rationale and was its own end. Ideations of atonement, substitution, purification, redemption, and the like were invented to explain the sacrifice once the ritual tradition was questioned. It was the break with the sacrificial traditions which gave rise to people's creative reflections about the reasons for the ritual in the first place.

2005); however, it is obvious that social transformation effected by ritual may bring with it concrete ramifications in terms of, among other things, social or material privilege.

This is not to say that emotions were not aroused during ritual, but Robertson-Smith emphasized the social utility of such emotions because they united worshippers with each other and with their totem-god(s) (e.g., 1957 [1889]:312–352).

By emphasizing the primacy of ritual, Robertson-Smith was reacting to his contemporary myth-and-ritualists of the opposite persuasion – those who saw myth as the heart of ritual, and ritual as, more or less, a performance of myth. Frazer was the most prolific of these. In a 12-volume treasury, Frazer explored a potpourri of myths of dying gods and dying kings and all measure of mythical aetiologies for ritual simulations of death and rebirth (1951 [1922]). Frazer's analysis was limited by his unilinear presumptions about the evolution of mental processes from magic (both homeopathic and contagious) to religion to science (1951 [1922]:59), but he matters here because he strove to thread a vast array of mythic elements into ritual practice, which he saw as ultimately meaningful.[32] In his intellectualist bent, he was continuing a trend associated with Tylor, who too saw "primitive" behavior as meaningful. Tylor endeavored to explore the felt presence of spirits among aboriginal peoples and showed the continued resonance of the notion of "the soul" into recent mentalities (1958 [1871]) (see the famous critique of both thinkers by Evans-Pritchard (1965[33])). The tension between the thinking of Robertson-Smith and that of his intellectualist contemporaries evolved into an ongoing argument concerning the primacy of the deed versus the word.

Few of the well-known ritual theorists of the twentieth century entirely discounted the imagination that might be triggered during ritual performance.

---

[32] For a cogent evaluation of Frazer's insights, see Stewart and Strathern (2014, chapters 2 and 3).

[33] For a defense of Tylor's thinking in its historical context, and particularly of his stress on embodiment, see Stewart and Strathern (2014, chapter 8).

Elements of Ritual and Violence

So, for instance, Van Gennep spurred a fascination with ritual symbols and latent meaning-production through his discussion of the liminality within rites of passage (1961), on which Victor Turner elaborated by developing a theory of the multivocality and dynamism of ritual symbols. Turner pointed to the imaginative excitement aroused by liminal states (e.g., threshold experiences wherein ritual participants were suspended between two different felt stages). In his view, such liminal states might occasion the birth of innovative concepts – dragons, for instance – out of discriminata drawn from more stable states (1974a, 1977 [n.b. 1977:68–71]). Fernandez too emphasized meaning production in rituals, finding them to be organized implicitly by metaphors. As he saw it, an inchoate and abstract subject – the ritual's "tenor" – assumed a more concrete and ostensive identity via the ritual "vehicle" – which is to say, via the performance (1972, 1977). That is, ritual performance effects a semantic transformation, predicating for the performer a new, more narrowly defined identity, albeit one already embedded in a system of associations. In a slightly different key, Geertz addressed the confusion of meaning in ritual when longstanding religious patterns met shifting social identities (1973:142–169). Ritual failure in Java was to be explained by the clash of the logico-meaningful cultural aspects of ritual patterns, which tended to perdure, with the causal-functional social aspects, which responded more immediately to historical change. The destabilization of meaning was triggered in part by the double-occupancy of ritual behaviors and meanings in religious and political spheres, e.g., reciting a Quranic prayer might affirm allegiance to a stable God and simultaneously to a volatile political party, leading over time to unpredictable commitments. Static constructions of ritual were incapable of addressing such destabilizations, so Geertz advocated a more dynamic approach (1973).

Ritualists who read this booklet cannot fail to recognize that this focus on ideation epitomized anthropological inquiry during the 1970s, when a predominant paradigm became semiotics (as opposed to, say, functionalism or Marxism). Speech codes and speaking behavior became ineluctable points of reference for understanding not only ritual but the whole of culture. Hence, Bateson observed a double-coded ritual semantics in the play-fighting of chimps (1972:180–181); Leach described metonymic substitutions (e.g., of cucumbers for cows) in Nuer offering processes which themselves were metaphorical; Levi-Strauss pondered the entirety of cultural meanings under the umbrella of linguistics, although he deepened the domain of linguistics by exploring speech's implicit infrastructure;[34] and Ricoeur brilliantly scrutinized the conditions that made meaningful social action possible through the lens of a language/discourse/inscription trichotomy (1973). Then Staal famously denied that ritual was language at all, but nonetheless stressed ritual syntax over semantics, finding ritual to predate language but to manifest an organizational structure emergent in language (1979); by implication, this organizational structure is perceived through the lens of language. Still today the lens of language is irresistible for some ritual theorists, as we see in a recent attempt to fathom ritual as a subjunctive, ideal mode of expression which defies and corrects the chaotic, broken, and indicative mode of everyday life, by Puett (2008:28–32). Puett relies for this on Orsi and a seminal essay by Victor Turner (1979). The language paradigm has been irresistible in ritual analysis.

Critics, though, attack language-based paradigms in ritual studies as too narrow, as a bias of our contemporary literary orientation and essentially as a fetishization of texts. According to some, equating ritual meaning with textual meaning is a historical reflex deriving from centuries of Christian exegesis which privileged inner script over outward behavior and correct belief over correct practice (Asad 1993). The proclaimed flaw is in decoding ritual behavior into propositional statements and/or poetics and in presuming an interiorized meaning which is other than the behavior itself. It should be noted that Asad's

---

[34] For summaries, see Stewart and Strathern (2014).

claimed Christian origin for the habit of privileging scripted models for reality is disputable, given the ancient Near Eastern practice of ritually inscribing or effacing texts in order to fix or break fate (Noegel 2010; Bottéro 2001:178). Apparently, the connection between the inscribed word and reality runs very deep in human imagination, as does the magical connection between special forms of ritual oratory (e.g., incantations, prayers) and fate.[35] Nonetheless, it is hard to dispute the weakness of the language paradigm for anthropological analysis. This paradigm has been noted since Geertz (1973). Although often held to account for emphasizing symbolism over embodied experience, Geertz recognized that anthropology was in practice a matter of identifying and then lifting meanings from the richer domain of lived experience, to be sewn together in the way of textural fabrics, or in the way of sentences and paragraphs. The end product is a kind of epiphenomenalism, with two layers of reality: one represented in text, and the other rooted in experience. Geertz recognized the hermeneutic limitations as well as the textual inevitability in anthropological analysis, which is why he advocated "thick description."

In the face of criticism against language paradigms in ritual studies, it is arguable that there well may be a certain inexorability to this reflexive association of ritual meaning with the kind of meaning that can be expressed in language. This is because the urge to speak may be correlated with the urge to formalize behavior into ritual expression. The notion that there *is* something that ritual formalizes, something to which it gives shape, is longstanding – from Tambiah's view of ritualization as communicating iconic paradigms of primordial events (1979) to Valeri's vision of ritual communication as intrinsically poetic (1985) (both discussed ahead). As is obvious by the very notion of ritual iconics or poetics, the expressive

---

[35] See Geller on the ideological coup of affixing prophetic texts to cosmic realities, and swaying opinion thereto, in the biblical context (2007).

potential of ritual action need not be equated solely with, say, logical propositions or myth. The gestural or deictic capacity of speech, the incho-ate nature of thought prior to speech, the craving to enunciate some experiences over others (experience not being flat), even the tendency to fantasize: all these would seem to relate not only to an impulse to speak but to an impulse to formalize behavior into recognizable shapes, which thereby become conspicuous and communicate through recognizable properties. The urge to formalize behavior via ritual and ceremony has been noted by Innis, who relies on Polanyi to point out that, "[w]ithout the ritual frame and our embodiment in it, our lives would be formless, 'submerged in a hundred cross-currents.' ... Just like the arts, rituals are 'imaginative representa-tions, hewn into artificial patterns; and these patterns, when jointly integrated with an important content, produce a meaning of distinctive quality'" (2005:209). If these "imaginative representations" and "meaning of distinctive quality" are intrinsic to human expression, it would seem artificial to separate ritual expression from other kinds of expression. Although dancing, costuming, and festive displays of various kinds all conceivably transcend propositional discourse, they still offer eloquent "meanings of a distinctive quality" to those who are primed to recognize them.[36]

It is Victor Turner who typically is credited with moving ritual theory away from discursive models as narrowly conceived in terms of propositional logic. He moved it instead toward what he called "comparative symbology" (1974). Comparative symbology allows for tensions between verbal and non-verbal symbols in ritual, art, affective feelings, values, and a creative flow in narrative imagination and cultural events (1974). This rich matrix linking various dimensions of ritual experience and expression seems obvious to us

---

[36] For a summary of the issues, see Kitts (2017b).

now. As noted in the section on ritual form, there is a significant literature evaluating these analytical trends.[37]

Ideation in Political Rituals

That ritual behavior can convey a message in a distinctive style is conspicuous in ritualized acts of political violence where ideation may loom large. Take the sensational cases of the 9/11 suicide activists and the recent self-immolations of Buddhist monks in the Tibetan region of China. On the surface, the latter group might seem explicitly ideological in its goals relating to the restoration of religious and political autonomy for Tibetans (however unstated, pending case), while the vehicle of self-burning leans on ritual precedent stemming back 15 or more centuries. Despite the general Buddhist mandate of noninjury to all life forms, the tradition of self-imposed bodily injury is exalted in the phantasmagoric, 2000-year-old Lotus Sutra, wherein the bodhisattva Medicine King is reported to have set fire to his body in homage to the buddhas (Benn 2007:4). Chinese Buddhist biographies and apocryphal sutras expand on this model by representing auto-cremating monks as heroically selfless, as newly minted bodhisattvas capable of conferring merit to other beings by their willing deaths. Supernatural response to these meritorious suicides of bodhisattvas is reputed to have included localized emissions of radiant colors and strange flights of birds. Biocosmic response to bodily mutilation is a notion deep in Buddhist lore in China, Japan, and also India (see Yu 2018, Stone 2018, and Ohnuma 2018). In sum, in the twenty-first century the communication of contemporary ideas, in many cases those of political protest, is amplified by archaic and traditional behaviors which to Western sensibilities might seem shocking forms of public self-torture.

[37] For overviews, see, e.g., Bell 1992, 1997, Strathern and Stewart 2010, Stewart and Strathern 2014, and the *Journal of Ritual Studies*, at www.pitt.edu/~strather/journal .htm.

While vastly different on the scale of harm, the 9/11 suicide activists also apparently had contemporary goals, given the symbolic targets of their destruction – namely, New York's World Trade Center and the Pentagon.[38] Yet they embraced what they conceived as ancient identities and ritual behaviors. We know that they assumed the names and mock-identities of early companions to the Prophet (Fouda and Fielding 2003:109) and that their Last Instructions referred to the attacks on the twin towers as a *ghazwa*, a raid, comparable to the early raids of the Medinan Muslims against the trading caravans which plied wares to the corrupt and polytheistic Meccans during the state-building period of Islamic history, between 622 and 632 (Kippenberg 2005; Kippenberg and Seidensticker 2006). Regarded by some Muslims as a golden age of spiritual guidance, this was a period when divine aid turned a number of early battles for Muslims against Meccan polytheists (see, e.g., Qur'an 8.9; 8.12–13; 8.17; cf. 3.124–126). As represented in their Last Instructions, the 9/11 participants imitated prebattle rituals to emulate this period. The instructions were initiated by a command to recite: "The Last Night. He said: one of the Companions said: the Messenger of God ordered us to recite it previous to a raid, and we recited it, took booty and were safe."[39] Since booty and safety could not possibly have been of consequence to planners of suicide, this ritualized recitation (three times reified by the model of an unknown "He," by one of the companions, by the messenger of God, and then imitated by the 9/11 activists themselves) surely served a nontangible aim, most likely the inculcation of a special state of mind and a sense of sanction through mimicry of primordial actors (Kitts 2010a). Recitation is of course a familiar theme in Islamic oral cultures anyway, stemming from preIslamic

---

[38] The author of the Last Instructions was careful not to mention political motives, however.

[39] Translation by Cook (2011).

Arabian poetic traditions through the first recitation imposed on Mohammed by the angel Gabriel on to the first and second Islamic pillars. Recitation was also prescribed in Instruction 6, which mandated reading/reciting the Quran, and implicitly in Instruction 12, which mandated expectorating Quranic verses from one's soul into one's clothing, papers, passports, and knife.[40] Similarly grounded in ancient rituals were the oath to die and the exhortation to purify the body (1."Mutual swearing of the oath to the death[41] and renewal of [one's] intention. Shave excess hair from the body and apply cologne. Shower."). While suicide is expressly forbidden in Islam (Afsaruddin 2018; Hafez 2018), it likely was rationalized here by the model of the battlefield deaths of ancient martyrs (Cook 2002, 2005). In any case, pledging one's life and purifying one's body before battle are common behaviors for Western holy warriors from Joshua through the Crusades,[42] and by mimicry surely conferred holy staging to the planned attacks. These are but a few of the preflight behaviors prescribed in the Last Instructions, a document setting out a whole set of ritual procedures meant conceivably to texturize the enactment of the attacks, as well as the perception of them by a select few.

Despite different modalities and goals, the behaviors of both the Buddhist monks and the 9/11 activists were violent in the basic sense of bodily injury (to selves, minimally), ritualized to replicate ancient traditions, and saturated with contemporary political motives. They can hardly be understood

---

[40] See Cook (2005) for the numbered order of the instructions. See Wlodarczyk (2009:88) and Ferme (2001: 2–3) on the ritualized manipulation of inscribed Qur'anic verses and associated powers in African traditions, specifically as used by combatants in Sierra Leone.

[41] The term is "bay`a li-l-mawt," an oath unto death. (Email to author from David Cook, November 24, 2009).

[42] See, e.g., von Rad 1958, 1991:41–42; Riley-Smith 1995:78–81, 83; Kippenberg 2005:36, nn18–20; Kitts 2010a:293–295, and cf. Quran 8:11.

without due consideration of ideas. By the thinking of Tambiah, Valeri, and others discussed ahead, similarly minded audiences will have recognized the juxtaposition of contemporary ideas with traditional behaviors in both of these instances, and will have responded, at least implicitly.

Lest such ideations and ritual theatrics seem designed only for the global stage, it should be noted that similar intertwining of ideational intent and heightened communicational register, albeit on a smaller scale, is found in strife-ridden pockets of contemporary small-band as well as ancient cultures. For instance, it is found among practitioners of assault sorcery (a.k.a. occult aggression) in culturally contested regions of Amazonia and New Guinea (Whitehead 2002, Stewart and Strathern 2004). There, situated at the interstices of traditional and newer justice systems, innovative assault sorcerers, also called shamanic or numinous warriors (Whitehead 2002:128ff), may combine ritual performance with explicit ideational intent in order to, for instance, inflict real or mystical injury on personal rivals and also on perceived representatives of hegemonic powers – whether traditional or evangelical Christian. Much like terrorist performance art (Juergensmeyer 2013), these mystical assaults, when known, have the effect of producing a heightened sense of foreboding and personal vulnerability for victims and witnesses. The violent intent, conveyed through rumors of rituals as well as through actual ritual enactments, is intentionally haunting and, in effect, socially destabilizing (cf. Tambiah 1996:221–243).[43] Comparable foreboding and fears of destabilization may be felt in ancient Near Eastern rituals too – for instance, in the ritualized killing of oath-victims (e.g., murdered sheep posing as prospective perjurers; Kitts 2011:237–38, 2015), in the violent smashing of inscribed texts and their

---

[43] The study of occult aggression has become something of a sensation in recent decades, the phenomenon being rooted in regions all over the contemporary world. For a summary, see Geschiere (2016).

implicated realities (Noegel 2010), or in the performed poetry of threat by some biblical prophets (e.g., Amos 7). Despite differences in scale and context, there are similar combinations of menacing ideas and elevated communicational registers among these various rituals. These speak to a conceivable enhancement of message and ominous force through ritualization.

Violent Imaginaries, Ritual Imaginaries

Related to these rituals' ominous expressions is the "violent imaginary." The violent imaginary is not typically associated with ritual studies, but rather is a relatively new rubric emerging out of research into the public impact of unanticipated, seemingly random, and frequent acts of violence.[44] Extralinguistic sensations – such as agitation, dread, sense of the uncanny – combined with fear, panic, as well as rumors and assumptions about the cosmological or political order, help to shape an imaginary, defined by Charles Taylor as "that largely unstructured and inarticulate understanding of our whole situation, within which particular features of our world become evident" and for which "practice largely carries the understanding" (2002:107). Such an unstructured and pre-articulate imaginary, with its overarching innuendos of menace, may precipitate an amorphous sense of social fragility and personal contingency among an affected population, leading to outbreaks of hysteria, conspiracy theory, and shifts in the very contours of perceived realities. A violent imaginary may be surmised to expand in public awareness alongside representations of danger, perversions of custom, and what Victor Turner regarded as liminoid breaks in our customary worlds (1974).

Being unstructured, a violent imaginary can be difficult to capture in analysis, but one striking attempt is offered by deBoeck, who describes the

---

[44] See, e.g., Schmidt and Schröeder 2001:9–13; Strathern and Stewart 2006; Aijmer 2000; Crapanzano 2004.

violent imaginary that dominated public focus in Kinshasa, DR Congo, in the 1990s (2005). In the wake of civil war, terror, HIV/AIDs, poverty, and other afflictions, Kinois society was reduced to a "realm of indistinction" (Mbembé's term 2002:267), with disintegrating boundaries between law and chaos, good and bad, the living and the dead, and other dichotomous frames of reference. A combustion of factors – the aforementioned cultural trauma, the influence of Jehovah's Witnesses, the millennial framework of the Book of Revelation, and novel practices of killing (from respun forms of mystical warfare to necklacing with burning tires) – generated both a real and an imagined necropolis, with apparent ghosts of the dead hovering not just at gravesites but also in streets, homes, churches, and nightclubs. Popular music and church services helped to channel and shape a feeling of impending menace in public imagination. Anticipating an end-times, Kinshasans felt suspended in what deBoeck identified as an "apocalyptic interlude" (2005:25), either already in or about to be in the final clasp of Satan. There was something palpable about this overhanging mood, as well as about the musical and ecclesiastical means of generating it.

Ritual can be a vehicle for conjuring a violent imaginary, as alluded earlier in the discussion of political rituals. Some ancient Western representations are especially illuminating because they explicitly convey menace. Biblical reports of the ritualized desecration of the bodies of war captives and/or internal competitors reflect what seems to have been an established ancient Near Eastern custom of corpse abuse (see, e.g., Olyan 2014, 2016). Similarly, dancing with disembodied enemy heads and/or publicly displaying them at feasts have been analyzed by historians of ancient Near Eastern art and literature as intentionally derisive (Collon 2003; Bahrani 2008; Noegel 2007, 2016) and meant to intimidate. One can imagine the trepidation of viewers.

Just as agonistically, although with more skin in the game, some early Christians planned their forthcoming martyr-spectacles to be not only to be imitations of Jesus, but also subversions of Roman notions of heroism (Streete

2018; Perkins 2002:31, 24, 36, 39, 40; Moss 2010). Their anticipated bloody performances functioned, rhetorically at least, as taunts. Hence, Ignatius wrote:

> Suffer me to be eaten by the beasts, through whom I can attain to God. I am God's wheat and I am ground by the teeth of wild beasts that I may be found the pure bread of Christ ... Then shall I be truly a disciple of Jesus Christ, when the world shall not see my body ... If I suffer I shall be Jesus Christ's freedman. (Ad Romanos 4.1–3, translated by Castelli 2004:79)

Designed at least in part for Roman tastes, the Christians' ostentatious sufferings, or hopes for them, repulsed especially the Stoics, who preferred more meditative, less theatrical forms of autothanasia (Perkins 2002:294). But the Christian aim was not the Stoics, but military *devotio* traditions with their heroic self-sacrifices, which the Christian martyrs aspired to simulate (Streete 2018). Perhaps curiously, once Christianity became accepted, Christian ritualized aggression remained evident in ritualized strategies to defang demons and everything that came with them, including demonic vapors. Christian exorcists were primed for battle, their rituals insinuating sovereign force over palpable enemies (Smith 2008; Kalleres 2014).

While restricted to early Western traditions, these examples illustrate a general pattern of enhancing menace through ritualization. They thereby support the idea that a violent imaginary may be generated by ritualized behavior.

It should be pointed out that ritual as a spur for violent imagination is not a new concept, as touched upon in Section I. Émile Durkheim (2001 [1915]) famously pondered the power of the Aboriginal corroboree to generate outbursts of violence along with feelings of transport and exaltation, which he named effervescence. For Durkheim, such experiences refreshed pre-existing ideas and images as if new; indeed, such experiences precipitated the birth of the very idea the sacred. Adolf Jensen (1963) studied the moment of imaginative seizure precipitated by certain violent rituals. For him the nascent epiphany arising from violent rituals did not have to be constructed entirely from scratch, but nonetheless might take on a new vitality during ritual experience. René Girard (1977) saw a conceivable soteriology as emerging spontaneously from violent scapegoating rituals, quite in addition to the unifying catharsis claimed to be the ritual's ultimate point. And, lately, Harvey Whitehouse (2004) has distinguished imagistic from doctrinal religious modes to sort out why some ritual experiences elicit life-changing revelations, whereas others merely reinforce the status quo. Suffice it to say that the evocative elements in ritual experience are ongoing items of analysis, and obviously related to a study of ritualized violence. It is fair to coin the phrase "ritual imaginary" to cover these evocative properties of ritual.

The Significance of Ritual Form

The other issue which must be addressed to grasp the intertwining of ritual and violence is ritual's formalization as behavior. This is indeed the focus of most contemporary ritual studies, although the rubrics for grasping this formalization tend to fluctuate among ritual communication, framing/meta-communication, embodiment, etc. Sketched in the next sections are some relevant themes and illustrations.

Ritual Formalization as Communication

That ritual communicates is probably its most accepted feature, despite questions about how it communicates. First it should be noted that ritual communication does not exclude speech acts *ipso facto*. Ritualized speech has been a subject of scholarly query since Austin (1975 [1962]), who pointed out that speech acts can be deeds when they have performative, or more explicitly perlocutionary, dimensions. Examples include "I dub thee knight," "I do thee wed," "[I] bless you," "I do swear," wherein, given proper circumstances, a knighting ceremony knights, a wedding vow weds, a blessing blesses, and an oath commits. This perlocutionary feature is related to the capacity of ritualized utterances to elicit conventions and to instantiate them in time, after which they may be perceived as socially binding. Discussion of the performative features of ritual speech extends into studies of oral contracts, word-magic, cursing, petitionary prayers, ritual calls, and more.[45] Note that all of these speech acts are far more than mere sound-puffs emitted from the mouth; instead they are understood to shift commitment on the part of the speaker and to elicit a shift in awareness by the hearer. These shifts extend beyond the simple conveyance of information; perlocutionary speech acts achieve palpable effects, such as establishing threats or binding speakers to a course of action.

Second, and at the other end of the speaking spectrum, some speech acts in ritual performance can suggest no semantics at all, but rather can be deictic, involving vocal pointing. Such pointing might include a battery of vocal phenomena such as calls, cries, melodies, and the use of obscure languages or terms devoid of contemporary semantics, but which nonetheless have a referencing function for audiences. Perhaps the most exotic example is glossolalia, which has been argued to elude vernacular representation and to point instead to a primordial unity which is ontologically prior to the conscious distinction between words and their referents, self and world, or body and mind. At least so it reputedly is understood by charismatic Catholics, for whom glossolalia

---

[45] Tambiah offered examples of this battery of verbal behaviors in 1968. Cursing traditions in antiquity have received a great deal of attention by, inter alia, Noegel 2010, Geller 2007, Eidinow 2007 (2010), and Kitz (2013). On ritual calls and their semantic loss, a striking example is Hittite *missa*, as explored by Stefanini in conjunction with Latin "mass" (1983).

ostensibly manifests a preBabel unity of the world's languages (Csordas 1990:26). Similarly, among the Indonesian Bugi glossolalia is said to manifest a sacred unity that existed before bifurcations such as male–female and differentiated spiritual realms (Becker 2004:105). In both cases, glossolalia without vernacular representation is thought to transcend the cultural logics captured and expressed by sentences, and to point instead to the mystical states attained by those who are vocalizing.

Such verbal acts and inarticulate vocalizations are only a small part of the spectrum of communication emphasized by the ritual-as-performance school, however. In Tambiah's pivotal essay of 1979, ritual was defined as a culturally constructed system of symbolic communication expressed in multiple media, patterned in its sequencing of words and acts, and exhibiting characteristics of formality (conventionality), stereotypy (rigidity), condensation (fusion), and redundancy (repetition) (1979:119). Thus, ritual action was not pointless show, but performative in three senses (1979:153; see also 1996:222), which oath-swearing happens to illustrate well. One is the Austinian sense outlined above, wherein a performance instantiates a convention – as when swearing an oath establishes a publicly recognized commitment. Second is an indexical sense, wherein ritual performance effects a shift in the performer's social status and ratifies it – as in committing a swearer to a promise which adheres to his public identity. Third is the staged sense, wherein multiple media enhance and intensify effects for performers and audiences – as when, in ancient times, the dramatic acts of publicly cutting the throat of an oath-victim and of witnessing his death signaled a commitment to the fate of perjurers for an assembly of spectators (my examples drawn from Homer and the ancient Near East). All of these elements continue to arouse discussion, particularly the staged sense, which in the ancient cases just referenced might evoke for the audience both sensory experience (e.g., an anticipatory shudder, dread) and frightful imagination (the specter of a painful death).

But Tambiah's most striking observation was his identification of ritual communication with pattern recognition and configurational awareness (1979:134). In perceiving familiar configurations of behavior, a ritual's audience recognizes the underlying shape of the performed behavior much as a viewer might intuit an underlying shape in an abstract work of art – say, the woman perceivable within Picasso's *Woman with a Mandolin*. Elsewhere I have paraphrased this as the recognition of Ur-forms, deeply rooted in cultural imagination and obliquely discernible through the prism of the immediate ritual performance (2012 [2005]). For Tambiah, the recognition was that of iconic analogues to primordial acts (1979:137) – not exactly iconic in the early Peircian sense, whereby the model and the primordial act share in a qualitative likeness,[46] but more than that. There is an underlying traditional shape which is iconicly envisioned through the performance in time.

Note the visual aspect to this kind of ritual communication. Tambiah's analysis did not entirely privilege the visual over other sensory dimensions (such as smell or touch), but the notion of iconic analogues in itself does imply visual, three-dimensional perception. For an audience already acquainted with it, this iconic kind of perception is rooted in a lived world of traditional choreography, pageantry, and titillating spectacles of all kinds. Visual recognition of such spectacles is arguably a-discursive, at least initially, based on what Susanne Langer pointed out decades ago. She argued that the visual arts communicate in their own terms, conveying tensions and resolutions through repetition and variation, relying on vehicles such as color, shape, and texture (1951:222–224). At the same time, art historians tell us that such tensions and resolutions are not strictly organic, but are complexly socialized (Morgan 2012)

---

[46] See Atkin (2013): http://plato.stanford.edu/entries/peirce-semiotics/

and that recognition of them can be gratifying on several levels, as illustrated by the masking traditions of the Loma of Guinea.

The extraordinary masking performances of the Loma of Guinea were described by the late Christian Kordt Højbjerg (2005, 2007). As he put it, the elaborate Loma masks all have histories and identities as divine figures, but in performance the maskers go beyond strict representation of these to invoke traditional oppositions – male–female, god–human, reality–illusion, Loma–Mandingo (language), secrecy–display, backward–forward (walking, speaking), life–death – through performance. Although these basic oppositions are customary and anticipated, maskers improvise and play on those oppositions, ritually innovating in order to present vibrant cultural re-hypostases. Some of these behaviors are designed to pervert received customs openly. For instance, some masks speak nothing but Mandingo, although Mandingo neighbors are disallowed from even witnessing Loma performances. Other maskers invert the rules of proper Loma speech by speaking backward. Some enter buildings walking backward. Some maskers conceal other masks and presumably identities within their clothing. For audiences in-the-know, the performances elicit a topsy-turvy imaginative world where traditional elements may be camouflaged or reconfigured to surprise and delight, and to trigger sudden recognitions of pre-existing cultural themes.

While on the one hand this ability to enact novel instantiations of pre-existing themes might seem a perfect example of what has been heralded as "habitus" (Bourdieu 1977, building on an essay by Mauss [1968]) and for that matter "a feel for the game" (Bourdieu 1977), the pleasing dimension of spectacular show speaks beyond habitus to established theories of ritual creativity and play. Many decades ago, Huizinga noted that some rituals can transport participants to what feels like an alternative sphere of experience (1950), to the delight of both actors and spectators. This coincides with Victor

Turner's analysis of public liminality and carnival, wherein performances can highlight taboo-breaking and even feigned menace (1979:484–486). The Loma masking performances are obviously carnivalesque. In the terms offered by Polanyi, they are "imaginative representations, hewn into artificial patterns," and produce a "meaning of distinctive quality" (Innis on Polayni, 2005:209) which titillates at multiple sensory levels. All this titillation hovers above an established set of social expectations, which the ritual actors gleefully pervert. These masking ceremonies show one creative instantiation of what Tambiah called a culturally constructed system of symbolic communication expressed in multiple media, patterned in its sequencing, and exhibiting characteristics of formality (conventionality), stereotypy (rigidity), condensation (fusion), and redundancy (repetition) (1979:119).

Rather than restrict figural recognition only to the visual and sensory, however, we should note that what Tambiah sees as iconic has also been understood as poetic. We have already decried a radical gulf between ritual models based on bodily experience versus on language, so it is worth a quick examination of Valeri's understanding of ritual as communicating on a paradigmatic axis in the model of poetics. This he opposed to the syntagmatic axis of propositional speech (1985:343). In the example of Loma masking (above), the paradigmatic recognition communicates through evocation, not straightforward exposition. What the masks and maskers evoke are deeply ingrained patterns or figures which transcend immediate context and elicit a reservoir of cultural imagination, which provides texture to the masking ritual in place.

Valeri's paradigmatic communication may be argued to proceed in the way of poetic figuration, in the sense illuminated by Ricoeur's treatment of metaphorical understanding. For Ricoeur, the poetic-visual gap is bridged when the figure of metaphor does not just supplant what it is supposed to represent, but actually confers figural shape on it and thus configures how we envision it (1981).

An example I have described elsewhere is Leviticus 26:36–37,[47] wherein the hypersensitive perception of a rustling leaf is made to resemble the perception of an enemy brandishing a sword (Kitts 2017a). Hearers are struck momentarily by the sword-like characteristics in the leaf, despite nominal incompatibilities; hence they anticipate sensory confusion, stumbling, and panic, followed by a fall. By creating a tension between tenor (here leaf) and vehicle (here sword), a metaphor may elicit awareness of a conceptual likeness which defies logical deduction and imposes shape on a particular understanding. By communicating along a paradigmatic axis in a particular time and circumstance, ritual performances too, like metaphors, may elicit likenesses which extend beyond immediate events and shape how those events are perceived.

The net point is that communicational models based on poetics and visualization need not be seen as antithetical. As Csordas put it, different domains of analysis may be complementary and may even come together in a kind of *rapprochement* when actual understanding takes place (2002:243).

Formality, Fixity, Rhythm, and Register

Primordial paradigms are not all that ritual communicates. It has been observed that just the formalism of ritual behavior can communicate an exceptional performance event. This has been described in terms of framing, patterning, semantic impoverishment, liturgical orders, register, and other rubrics.[48] The

---

[47] "As for those of you who are left, I will make their hearts so fearful in the lands of their enemies that the sound of a windblown leaf will put them to flight. They will run as though fleeing from the sword, and they will fall, even though no one is pursuing them. They will stumble over one another as though fleeing from the sword, even though no one is pursuing them. So you will not be able to stand before your enemies" (NIV translation).

[48] Of the usual features of ritual, Maurice Bloch, for instance, identifies degrees of formality, patterning, repetition, and rhythm (2010:21). Roy Rappaport identifies

paragraphs that follow summarize some interrelated features which have been claimed to distinguish ritual communication from everyday communication and which may cast light on how ritual behavior can serve violent intent.

Formality in ritual is gauged traditionally by its relatively fixed patterning of behavior, by its performance rhythms, and by its heightened performance register. Fixity implies predictability, however relative. Typically, we think of fixity in terms of a known sequence of behaviors whose coherence is essential for identifying the ritual and the custom it enacts, if any. Rhythmically speaking, familiar ritual movements tend to be punctuated by pauses and distinguished by pacing. In fact, ritual formality has been compared to music. Ritual movements utilize a kind of melody (the sequence), punctuated by rhythm (pacing) and by recognizable refrains (e.g., known symbolic gestures). Catholic genuflection and Islamic prayer are simple cases in point; the sequence of movements identifies the ritual (its melody); its pacing, with stress at the finale of genuflection and at the submissive gesture in Islamic prayer, shows its rhythm; and both can include a refrain – their respective hand-gestures, for instance – and can function as refrains within larger sequences of formalized behavior. Obviously this model is especially apt for rituals which actually involve music, but the model has wider application.

Ritual fixity, according to Rappaport, serves longevity, in that fixity is tied to resistance against structural change over the vagaries of time. A number of performance conditions – proper place, authority, time, and circumstance, etc. – support this resistance to change, but perhaps the most important factor is

ritual encoding by someone other than the performers, formality, degree of invariance, and metaperformative qualities, by which he meant the way that a ritual's performance establishes the conventions it enacts (1999:32–50). I have summarized these as patterning/sequencing, rhythm, condensation, and formality/register in another essay (2011).

audience response. According to Rappaport, audiences respond to ritual performances on a scale of increasing formality and decreasing spontaneity
(1999:34; 1966:428; Bloch 1974, 1975:6–13). At least in the most theatrical of
rituals, formal and constrained movements compel the attention of audiences,
communicate an intangible sense of power and traditional sanction, and dis-
courage open challenge of the convention enacted. Consider again a Catholic
Eucharistic service. The degree of behavioral formalization in the offering and
accepting of the host marks off, or frames, the ritual pattern communicated in
church from the patterns of ordinary communication. With or without
a complete awareness of church doctrines, congregations comprehend that
they are witnessing a sober and traditional event, and their responses may be
keyed for the stature of that event. Contrast a priest distributing the host during
a mass to, for instance, a parent handing out cookies in the kitchen.
Formalization helps to encrypt the ritual as a hallowed event. High formalization is tantamount to register, which is arguably proportional to the ritual's
depth of tradition and likely communicative impact.

In some rituals the intended elevating of register is unmistakable and
transparent. Among rituals which transparently convey a threat of violence, the
high register and dramatic features may communicate an overt shock-and-awe
quality. Allusions to this quality were made in our earlier discussion of a ritual
imaginary, but ancient oaths illustrate the issue of register quite well.
Elsewhere, I have discussed in detail the specter of gasping, dying lambs in
the oath-sacrifice cementing a truce between the Achaeans and Trojans in Iliad
3 (2005 (2012):100–114; 2011:238). Conjoined with spilled wine representing
the spilled brains of perjurers as well as curses promising the same for their
families, the close focus on the dying lambs likely compelled the attention of
audiences to oath-sacrifices, as well as of audiences to the poetic performances
of this Homeric scene. It would be hard to miss the threat to bodily well-being
enacted in such displays. Based on similarly dramatic acts described on ancient

Near Eastern treaty tablets, we may presume that ritualized cruelty was part of the ancient Near Eastern *koinē* for oaths. Consider, for instance, these ancient oath-curses and representations of punishments for violating oaths:

> Just as the *Cursers* sinned against Bel and he cut off their hands and feet and blinded their eyes, so may they annihilate you, and make you sway like reeds in water; may your enemy pull you out like reeds from a bundle. (Parpola and Watanabe 1988: 57, sec. 95)

> May [the gods] [slaughter] you, your women, your brothers, your sons, and your daughters like a spring lamb and a kid. (Parpola and Watanabe 1988:57, sec. 96A)

> Uaite', together with his armies, who had not kept the oath (sworn) to me, who had fled before the weapons of Assur, my lord, and had escaped before them, – the warrior Irra (the pest god) brought them low. Famine broke out among them. To (satisfy) their hunger they ate the flesh of their children. Every curse, written down in the oath which they took, was instantly visited (lit. fated) upon them by Assur, Sin, Shamash, Adad, Bel, Nabu, Ishtar of Nineveh, the queen of Kidmuri, Ishtar of Arbela, Urta, Nergal (and Nusku). The young of camels, asses, cattle and sheep, sucked at seven udders (lit. suckling mothers) and could not satisfy their bellies with the milk. The people of Arabia asked questions, the one of the other, saying: "Why is it that such evil has befallen Arabia?" (And answered), saying: "Because we did not keep the solemn (lit. great) oaths sworn to Assur; (because) we have sinned

against the kindness (shown us by) Assurbanipal, the king
beloved of Enlil's heart. (Luckenbill 1968, sec. 828)

In no way barren is the oath and the blood of lambs,
the unmixed libations and the right hands in which we trusted.
For if the Olympian does not fulfill it at once,
he will fulfill it later, and with might he will avenge it
with their heads and their wives and also their children.

(Iliad 4.158–162)[49]

The transparent menace in these curses speaks to their intended impact, or, as earlier described, their ritual imaginary.

Not all ritual menace is so transparent, however. Rituals based on opaque rather than transparent dynamics may rely for communicative force on a more subtle suggestion of mystery and/or danger, grasped only by those who are immersed in the culture and in the ritual imaginary. A well-studied example is the ritual dances performed by masked, male members of secret Poro societies among the Sierra Leone's Mende (aka Mande) peoples. In some cases, dancers are known to wear enfolded squares of Quranic verses (written in Arabic, which few people can actually read) concealed behind their costumes and against their bodies (Wlodarczyk 2009:88–89). During performance, a kind of spiritual combustion is thought to result from the contact between the animating human body and the activating power transmitted by the concealed words and substances, so that masked performers are known on occasion to lose control, attack bystanders, and seize property with impunity. To add to the complexity, Poro costuming is in itself a way of concealing and revealing power. Masking, cross-dressing, and the wearing of amulets traditionally have

---

[49] My translation.

played key roles in the region's wars, and are thought to channel a hidden realm of material power residing underneath the visible world (Ferme 2001:1–4; Wlodarczyk 2009:27–31, 89–91; Ellis 1995:193–194). During the civil wars of the 1990s, for instance, the wearing of ronko jackets – charm-encrusted garments transformed by esoteric manufacturing rituals – was expected to wrap protection from harm around warriors entering the zone of death, in this case battle (Richards 2009:504). This mirrored a similar custom for the newly dead, for whom a ritually manufactured funeral shroud was thought to slow bodily disintegration for persons transitioning from the world of the living into the unpredictable world of spirits (Ferme 2001:54; Richards 2009:504). For the warriors, it was not simply the wearing of the garment which deterred harm; the garment and its wearer first had been bonded together through initiation rituals (Richards 2009:505; Wlodarczyk 2009:85–91; Ellis 1995:188–189). The empowering strategies of such rituals, as shown in the complex Mende case, draw on the ambiguous relationship between concealed powers and the superficial expressions which both hide and suggest them (Ferme 2001:162). The audience enculturated to appreciate these themes will perceive the potential menace, although that menace is likely to elude those who do not understand the significance of secrecy in Mende societies. The communication of register in such a case obviously will lean on a particularized ritual imaginary.

Semantic Impoverishment and Amplification of Message

As inferred from the Sierra Leonean examples above, despite the communicative aims of ritual performances, what rituals communicate is not always semantically precise. Whereas everyday speech offers tools for the reciprocal give-and-take and mutual refinement of ideas during conversation, ritual oratory is said to lack the versatility in vocabulary, syntax, tonality, loudness, illustration, speech act sequencing (Bloch 1975:13), and presumably also pacing and gesture. Except in the complicated case of spontaneous rituals touched upon ahead the prescribed features and behavioral restrictions of ritual performances are said to serve tradition, which typically is built upon enacting precedent rather than upon arguing with it. New meanings, if any, are negotiated through contextual variations, and rarely invented outright. Perhaps ironically, semantic impoverishment can serve the amplification of message.

One popular rubric for pondering this amplification has been framing. In a theory of play and fantasy, Bateson pioneered the concept of ritual framing in terms of metacommunication. That is, by its formalization, a ritual communicates by itself that "this is ritual" *ipso facto*, regardless of any particular ritual paradigms or content involved. The frame carries its own message. However, by simultaneously addressing the ambiguous interstices between a ritual frame's interior and exterior – such as denotation, threat, paradox – Bateson also launched a discussion of the frame's "fuzziness" (1972:177–193) and its inadequacy as a rubric for capturing the whole of ritual, or of play for that matter. This weakness has been pursued in recent decades by Handelman and others who investigate the ritual frame for its likeness to a Moebius ring (n.b., Handelman 2005:578–581), wherein inner content and outward frame are not consistently distinct and indeed twist inside and out within each other. As shown below, metacommunication cannot prevent miscommunication, or even rejection of the frame itself.

Some relatively straightforward illustrations of the strengths and weakness of the metacommunicative paradigm, and also of ritual's semantic impoverishment, are our earlier examples of the Buddhist auto-cremations and the 9/11 suicides. As noted, both examples rely on authoritative paradigms as inscribed in literature (the Lotus Sutra and Chinese hagiographies; Quranic sura and the hadiths) to evoke tradition, and the targeted audiences are expected to recognize the underlying paradigms (or frames) right through the prism of the immediate event. However, because these underlying paradigms lack semantic precision, what the rituals communicate is not always so unambiguous. Paraphrasing Valeri, it is because of the lack of precision that, even though audiences to a ritual may recognize the underlying frame, they also may dispute its relevance to the moment and the perfection of the performance that goes with it (1985:342). This harks back to Geertz's analysis of the performative ambiguity stemming from the clash of logico-meaningful cultural patterns with the causal-functional social aspects of ritual performances (Geertz 1973). Semantic impoverishment can enhance ritual communication, but also can render it depleted of significance to those for whose eyes the ritual is cast. Hence, many Buddhists are horrified at the auto-cremations and dispute underlying prototypes, while the vast majority of Muslims have denied the would-be heroism of the 9/11 activists, seeing their efforts as perverting rather than performing ancient rituals.

A number of contemporary scholars have pondered the skewed nature of contemporary violent acts and the potential for miscommunication. For instance, sociologist Bernhard Giesen might see the Buddhist auto-cremations and the 9/11 attacks as third-order ritual events, set apart from the first-order (originating sacred moments) and second-order events (staged repetitions of the first) by the oblique performance shape and conceivably distorted context of the contemporary situation (Giesen and Suber 2005. Even nonviolent ritual acts may fail, as Ronald Grimes has noted in his treatment of infelicitous performances (1990). These are basic problems of ritual hermeneutics.

Ritual's Seductive and Somatic Qualities

Notwithstanding a certain degree of hermeneutic opaqueness, ritual's constellation of formality, register, and semantic depletion, when a fortuitous confluence, may be said to make for ritual's seductive quality. The level of seduction might be compared, again, to music. Bloch compared ritual persuasion to a song since, rather than argue with a song, the typical response is to surrender to it (1974:15, 55–81; 1975:6–13). Radcliffe-Brown pointed out about music within ritual that "[a]ny marked rhythm exercises upon those submitted to its influence a constraint, impelling them to yield to it and to permit it to direct and regulate the movements of body and even those of the mind" (Radcliffe-Brown 1964:249, as referenced in Tambiah 1979:113; Rappaport 1999:226–228). The comparison of ritual to music is endorsed by evolutionary anthropologists Alcorta and Sosis, who tell us that both music and ritual stimulate neurophysiological responses which intensify experience,[50] kindle emotions,[51] and promote social bonding. Richards points out that song may be manipulated ritually not only to entrain emotions and movements, but

[50] "Music has important neurophysiological effects. As a 'rhythmic driver,' it impacts autonomic functions and synchronizes 'internal biophysiological oscillators to external auditory rhythms'. The coupling of respiration and other body rhythms to these drivers affects a wide array of physiological processes, including brain wave patterns, pulse rate, and diastolic blood pressure. This 'coupling effect' has been shown to be present in humans at a very early age. Music amplifies and intensifies this effect through the use of instruments, or 'tools,' thereby providing a means of synchronizing individual body rhythms within a group. Recent work by Levenson has shown that synchronized autonomic functions, including such things as pulse rate, heart contractility, and skin conductance, are positively and significantly associated with measures of empathy" (Alcorta and Sosis 2005:336 [internal citations omitted]).

[51] "The ability of religious ritual to elicit both positive and negative emotional responses in participants provides the substrate for the creation of motivational communal symbols. Through processes of incentive learning, as well as classical and contextual conditioning, Ronkothe objects, places, and beliefs of religious ritual are invested with emotional significance. The rhythmic drivers of ritual contribute to such conditioning through their 'kindling effects'" (Alcorta and Sosis 2005:337). "Like the phonemes, words, and sentences of language, the use of musical instruments to produce sounds permits the combining of such sounds to create emotionally meaningful signals. These, in turn, can be arranged and rearranged within

to stimulate social solidarity against the overt wishes of some participants. His example is the singing forced upon captives taken by the RUF during the 1990s conflict in Sierra Leone and Liberia. The pointed goal of the singing was to promote bonding between abductees and abductors, but also, secondarily, to suppress abductees' horror in the face of the abductors' atrocious acts (Richards 2007:72).

Arguably, singing rituals have been exploited to seductive effect in many conflicts, presumably because the engagement created by shared rhythms and also melodies is thought to penetrate human sociality at a deeper level than do explicit ideologies or even common symbologies (granted that the impacts of music, ideology, and symbol may be hard to separate in actual experience). Richards explains the musical dynamic in terms of the phenomenological concept of intentionality, whereby any perceiving subject is already engaged with the world before s/he distinguishes discernible content: "Musical performance is *unassigned* intentionality. . . . response to music involves pulse-following behaviour, invokes memory and creates a sense of anticipation . . . but is not specifically 'about' anything" (Richards 2007:76–77). Many examples of seductive singing during conflict could be cited: "Bella Ciao" among the partisans in World War II, "Lili Marlene" among the World War II Axis as well as Allied forces, Simon Bikindi's Hutu hate songs during the Rwandan civil conflict of the 1990s, etc. Whatever else it sought to accomplish, singing together in wartime surely promoted some degree of solidarity. In kinship with music, ritual's performative dimensions, because they are also rhythmic and communal, are argued to engage

encompassing musical structures. The formality, sequence, pattern, and repetition of such musical structures themselves elicit emotional response through their instantiation of ritual. Music thereby creates an emotive 'proto-symbolic' system capable of abstracting both the signals and structure of ritual" (Alcorta and Sosis 2005:339).

attention, dominate focus, entrain bodily response, and thus to be persuasive, even against a participant's will (Alcorta and Sosis 2005; Richards 2007).[52]

Musical and ritual seduction thus is tied to somatic experience. Within the last few decades, studies of the ritual body have triggered a focus not only on the socialized dimensions of corporeality, as might pertain, for instance, to Bourdieu's *habitus*,[53] but more basically on rhythm, dance, pain, pleasure, trance, emotional arousal, and the transformation of consciousness through extraordinary events. An advantage of this focus on the somatic is not only that it allows consideration of nonhuman ritualists – birds, obviously, have rituals too – but that it allows us to contemplate kinetic and visceral dimensions to ritual experience. These persuade at a level typically held to be beneath thought, although not necessarily estranged from thought. Mark Johnson deems musical persuasion deeper than sentences precisely because its meaning is rooted in the flow and rhythm of bodily experience, tied to our deepest experience of being alive (2007:236).

However, it is not as if embodiment eludes imagination, either. Instead, embodiment is argued to be the basis for imagination. Once unfashionable, privileging the body as a site for meaning production and imagination has been promoted defiantly by Lakoff (1980, 1999[54]), Johnson (1987, 2007), Bryan Turner (1992), and Csordas (1990, 2002), some of whom constructed their theories on top of existential phenomenology as articulated

---

[52] However, such seductions are not always successful. In the case of song, for instance, resistance may take the form of singing another, competing song (reviewer for Kitts 2017a).

[53] Catherine Bell famously harvested Bourdieu's notion of *habitus* to emphasize the creation of special space–time modalities through the ritual body, and emphasized the circularity of empowerment on and by ritual agents, among other things (1997).

[54] Surprisingly, there are some overt neurally reductive elements in parts of Lakoff and Johnson's 1999 *Philosophy in the Flesh*.

by Merleau-Ponty and Heidegger. Bodily virtuality – e.g., our up–down axis, our reliance on the hand – has been argued to be foundational in shaping imagination and meaning (Bryan Turner 1992:117–119).[55] Csordas's analysis is particularly intriguing. Distinguishing the body itself from embodiment and making embodied experience – the lived body – "the starting point for analyzing human participation in a cultural world"(2002 [1993]:241), Csordas builds on Merleau-Ponty, Bourdieu, and Schutz to describe a somatic mode of attention which is key to grasping ritual healing. Merleau-Ponty had started his analysis of human experience with perception – in his view, always already embedded within a world; perception is never without its object. Bourdieu had seen perception as socially informed, as incorporating the social world somatically, but he also saw that we constitute our worlds through practice. Schutz, and for that matter Merleau-Ponty too, analyzed the sharpening of attention when figures emerge from an indeterminate horizon of awareness; as we turn toward them, we constitute the figures as distinct to us; this turning, this distinguishing, says Csordas, is an embodied act. Building on these notions, Csordas describes our "culturally elaborated ways of attending to and with one's body in surroundings that include the embodied presence of others" (2002 [1993]:244). It is with the tools of somatic understanding that Csordas can describe the experience of ritual healers in embodied terms, not as "trance," out-of-body experiences, or psychosis (imposed terms all), but as heaviness, tingling, distinct smell, vibrations, or *espiritismo* – which is to say seeing, hearing, or feeling spirits (2002 [1993]:246–249). Embodiment and imagination become close to indistinguishable in somatic modes of analysis. Cartesian dualisms fail to apply.

[55] Cognitivists go even further to argue that we are evolutionarily primed to see eyes, faces, bilateralism, up–down axes, and other anthropomorphisms in other creatures and even in inanimate things (Guthrie 2007).

Embodied imagination is striking in a number of ritual contexts, but particularly in those involving music and dance, as already alluded. Ethnomusicologist Dissanayake describes the ability of traditional music to conjure visitations by extraordinary beings. The Brazilian Kalapalo sing such beings into existence, while the Nigerian Yoruba dance them into existence (2006:33). Friedson describes cross-rhythmic drumming during healing rituals among the Tumbuka people of Malawi: the rhythms engender the immediate sensation of something entering and leaving the body for participants and audiences alike (1996). Similarly, Becker describes an all-night drumming event to exorcise demons during the Sri Lankan Yak Tovil: the drumming intensifies until the rhythms, formerly metric, become nonmetric and speech-like, then demons appear and the patient and audience both feel "hit with sound." Finally, the patient dances with the demon until collapsing, as the demon departs (2004:32–34). Similarly to Tumbuka healing rituals, the Yak Tovil is a multisensory and multi-media event which elicits "deep listening." This begins, Becker suspects, at a precognitive level in the brain, before it expands to involve memory, feeling, and imagination (2004:29). In a similar vein, Friedson acknowledges that the musical structure in Ewe cross-rhythmic drumming can take on the "*force vitale* of a saturated and animated engagement with the world" (2009:188).

Ritual Imagination Violently Performed

The propensity for ritual seduction, through music or otherwise, is ostensibly most acute among youths and young adults, which is the same demographic solicited to be members of paramilitary groups in conflicts world round (Stewart and Strathern 2002:29). As Alcorta and Sosis show, adolescents tend to be especially responsive to the emotional valencing induced by participation in such rituals. High-intensity rituals involving pain and bodily risk are likely to be found among groups of nonrelated individuals who engage in intermittent high-risk cooperative endeavors, such as external warfare (Alcorta and Sosis 2005:349). The reader may reflect back on initiation rituals among the Kamajors, already discussed. The Hutu Interahamwe ("to launch together") are another conspicuous case. This was the militia of closely bonded youths responsible for the majority of genocidal killings and maimings during the 1994 conflict in Rwanda (Taylor 1999:33, 178). I have not been able to uncover any ritualized means of inducting youths into the Interahamwe,[56] except for their reputed dancing to the popular hate songs of Simon Bikindi, who combined traditional and military dress in staged musical exhortations to kill.[57] (Musical rituals need not always be incendiary, of course.) With or without the musical incitement, the Interahamwe's paramilitary activities were outstanding examples of ritual seduction combined with the ritual imaginary, as suggested by Christopher Taylor's analysis (1999).

In his structuralist-leaning analysis, Taylor saw the violent behaviors of the Interahamwe as implicitly enacting centuries-old notions about the royal body as a cosmic conduit for fecundating liquids (*imaana*) flowing on the land, and enacting too the symbolic forms in which that flow might be obstructed, as well as archaic means for overcoming that obstruction. Traditionally, in times of crisis, such overcoming was managed by regicide or by shedding sacrificial blood at auspicious boundaries (Taylor 2013, Stewart and Strathern 2002:31–32). As a bipolar field of meaning,[58] the

[56] For initiation rituals in paramilitary groups in Liberia, Sierra Leone, and Uganda during the same decade, see Wlodarczyk 2009: 83–91 and Ellis 1995:188–192.

[57] Bikindi was later found guilty of incitement to genocide: www.nytimes.com/2002/03/17/magazine/killer-songs.html.

[58] "Notice, therefore, that the noun *isibo* and its root verb *gusiba* appear to encompass two apparently contradictory meanings. One field of meaning seems to center on living beings in movement. Another set of meanings seems to crystallize around the ideas of obstruction and loss. A single verbal concept in Kinyarwanda thus appears to

flow/blockage symbolism continues to penetrate contemporary healing practices in Rwanda, as it penetrated older ritual practices relating to agriculture and national polity. According to Taylor, the violent acts of the Interahamwe youths were underwritten by this flow/blockage symbolism. The Interahamwe "blocked flow" not only by damming rivers and blocking roads, but by symbolically and concretely preventing the free movement of bodies and of bodily fluids. In a concrete sense, the Interahamwe inhibited movement by cutting the legs, feet, and Achilles' tendons of Tutsi humans as well as of their cattle. They blocked symbolic flow by castrating men, debreasting women, and impaling both men and women. They simulated the releasing of blocked flow by shedding blood, as in hacking Tutsis to death at roadblocks on major thoroughfares as well as on narrow footpaths (Taylor 1999:99–150). The traditional bipolar field of meaning of blockage and flow is argued to have shaped the methods of killing implicitly, conferring a ritualized quality to the killings. While the shared and emplaced reality that Bourdieu called *habitus* might bear on the unacknowledged persistence of the alternating thematic of blockage and flow, the very dramatic actualizations of this blockage and flow symbolism attest as well to the grip of a ritual imaginary – namely, in the replication of formalized killings and healings tied to failed kings, from whom the flow of *imaana* to the people had ceased.

This is not to say that there was nothing political about these torturous acts. No doubt the youths presumed that their behavior was primarily political, but torture's symbolic and ritualized dimensions have been recognized as cutting across political dimensions in a variety of contexts (Taussig 1984,

encompass the idea of flow and its opposite, the idea of blockage. Furthermore, in this second instance, this notion of 'blockage' is related to the idea of doing harm to someone" (Taylor 1999:125).

1987; Malkki 1995).[59] As Jeffrey Alexander notes about terrorism, such performances have latent and manifest symbolic references. Background structures of immanent meaning combine with particular, contingent goals in the way that conflicts are narrated and choreographed, in how they are made to cross sacred, profane, and mundane spheres of life, and in how they define actors, drama, and catharsis. He sees such terroristic performances as dramaturgical (2004:91, citing Goffman 1967[60]).

The above referenced symbolic locations (e.g., rivers, roadblocks) and symbolic behaviors (e.g., blocking and freeing the flow of vital liquids, including blood) alert us to another important aspect of ritual performance, related to the ritual imaginary. This is the concrete way that ritual practices may imprint behavior and memory. Fernandez (1977) coined the phrase "ritual leitmotif'" for implicitly ritualized habits which persist even outside of formal settings, but nonetheless communicate themes associated with ritual conventions, albeit *pars pro toto*. I have argued elsewhere that, at least in Homeric poetry, strong emotions may be poetically extended into ritual leitmotivs, as when the anger signified by the word *kholos* is poetically extended into the ritual leitmotif for *poinē*, retribution or exchange. The leitmotif of retribution elicits associations with a range of angry motivations and helps to shape the character of Achilles in the Iliad. Ritual leitmotifs may occur in the form of facsimiles of more formalized ritual behaviors (i.e.,"ritual-lite"), or when an array of details associated with ritual behavior coalesces and all at once elicits the broader ritual tradition through sudden metaphorical transference (Kitts 2010b). At least the first of these arguably occurred in the Rwandan context when the Interahamwe undertook to kill Tutsis in such a way as to mimic the releasing and blocking of

---

[59] Both trauma and torture are argued to intrude into awareness at a level beyond signification but to be persistent in affect (Crapanzano 2004:91).

[60] Goffman, reproduced in Grimes 1996:268–278.

flow by cutting the breasts and Achilles' tendons of Tutsi people and cattle. A perceptive audience to these acts would have recognized the ritual leitmotivs and grasped their underlying complications. The shaping of killing behavior by ritual form may lend to the behavior a certain hallowed quality, although such hallowing is likely to elude witnesses unfamiliar with the underlying traditions.

Ritual Spontaneity and Elevated Register

Ritual spontaneity may seem a contradiction in terms, but considering the performative dynamics of the Interhamwe youths, it appears that their behavior was not only texturized by hallowed traditions, but also by their elevated register. That is to say, the youths not only simulated deep cultural themes, but they enacted them as ad hoc ritualizations. Presuming that the first killings by individual members of the Interahamwe elicited at least an initial shudder (in many cases the Tutsi and Hutu were neighbors), it is not a leap to attribute an elevated register to their subsequent displays of deliberate, formalized cruelty with overtones of revenge. One needn't be a depth psychologist to grasp this; the heightened register is obvious by the methodical deliberation and extreme nature of the destructive acts. For instance, it is clear by the cuttings of Achilles' tendons, even those of cattle, and by the impalings of Tutsi people that these were meaning-laden cruelties, and not simple, instrumentally efficient eliminations of rivals.

It may not be a leap also to attribute a ritualized nuance, albeit coupled with dread, to the murderous acts forced upon fleeing Hutus, some of whom were required to bludgeon captive Tutsis before passing Interahamwe roadblocks (Taylor 1999:131). In the experience of the fleeing Hutus, Whitehouse sees a similarity to the experience of reluctant novices in violent initiation rituals (2004:126), for whom a moment-by-moment hyper-awareness during violent acts might raise the register of what occurs, and seal the ritually induced trauma indelibly into memory. Along the same lines, Stewart and Strathern have described an enhanced now-time during ritualization (2014; chapter 9). We have all participated in faux-rituals. The line between faux and the vivid present is conceivably porous in situations of great stress.

Ritual Emotion, Texture, and Intentionality

The hallowing of emotion through leitmotivs and also through more fixed performances contradicts the tendency, attributed to ritual by some impressive analysts, for the emotionally distancing effect of ritual performances (Rappaport 1999:123; Langer 1951:123–124; Tambiah 1979:124). Typically, ritual is thought to constrain emotion, to give play to stereotypical simulations of emotions (Rappaport 1999:24), and "to establish conventional understandings, rules, and norms, in accordance with which everyday behavior is *supposed* to proceed" (Rappaport 1999:123). It is inarguable that this holds true for some very formal ritual ceremonies. But those classical theories emphasize formal communication at the expense of the immediacy of ritual experience for individual participants. As noted earlier, Alcorta and Sosis have tracked the capacity of ritual to excite emotions and entrain autonomic motivational states, generating lasting impressions and evoking meaningful symbolic networks (2005:336–337). Indeed, they see the connection between emotional states and the abstractions tempered by symbolic performances as lying at the heart of religious experience.[61] Whitehouse's description of the imagistic mode of ritual also attempts to take into consideration the lasting impact of ritually induced, life-changing excitements (2004) which reverberate into other spheres of life. Particularly in rituals

[61] "Human use of ritual to conditionally associate emotion and abstractions creates the sacred; it also lies at the heart of symbolic thought. The brain plasticity of human adolescence offers a unique developmental window for the creation of sacred symbols. Such symbols represent powerful tools for motivating behaviors and promoting in-group cooperation" (Alcorta and Sosis 2005:348–349).

which either simulate violence or launch it (such as oaths), it is difficult to imagine an emotionally distancing effect, except insofar as immediate violence may be delayed through the use of symbolic substitutes (such as killed lambs). Nonetheless, an immediate, raw, emotionality might be expected to prevail during, say, oaths to exact vengeance.

It is conceivably possible to break down the emotionality in ritual to first- and second-order expressions, wherein the first order is irresistibly compelling, while the second is filtered into symbolic actions, along the lines of Giesen's analysis of ritual performances mentioned earlier. Yet such a separation might seem artificial when one examines certain actual evidence. Taylor's examples of ritualized hacking are obvious cases in point: symbolic behavior can be perfectly vehement, even if – or especially if – ritually staged. The dramatic register may signal emotional intensity and deliberate intent. In any case, it would be a mistake to deny emotion in ritual, particularly in rituals which enact violence or lead to it.

Lastly, related to the study of ritual leitmotivs, and emotion's extension into them, is the matter of ritual texture. Understanding ritual performance as a symbolic form of communication, I have drawn this notion of texture from Ricoeur's analysis of metaphor, and more particularly of the verbal texture generated by a metaphorical string of words and "co-extensive to the verbal structure itself" (Ricoeur 1981:244). Applying the notion of ritual texture to emotion, what this means is that not just any ritual form will do justice to the expression of strong emotion, whether joyous or murderous. Consider the way that overwhelming joy may induce one to dance a jig, rather than, say, a tango. The jig may be deemed the ritual texture generated by joy, and to shape the expression of joy differently than would a tango. At the other end of the emotional spectrum, rage too generates its own textures, which of course will vary in accord with traditional constraints. In the Homeric case mentioned above, the ritual leitmotif of *poinē*, retribution, is texturized, at least in poetry, by the emotion of *kholos* (Kitts 2010b). But given the seeming ubiquity of the urge for revenge in human societies, we can assume that the emotional and ritual textures of rage will manifest quite differently across traditions.[62]

In this discussion of ritual, we must note too that the rooting of ritual expression at the site of emotions has phenomenological implications, as alluded to in the discussion of music, above. Ritual presumes engagement on the part of participants. In his study of Sri Lankan sorcery, Bruce Kapferer asserts that ritual practitioners presume intentionality in the ontological sense described by Husserl and Sartre. From the sorcerer's point of view, our sensitivity to ritual manipulations is fundamental to our status as beings in the world. Ritualized behaviors aim for effect at the dynamic joining of the human body and a lifeworld. Drawing on Sartre, Kapferer points out that this is a magical joining where human beings meet other human beings in a space where they also individuate themselves (1997:1–8). The meeting of self and other is intrinsically paradoxical and also risky. Open to ritual manipulations, the sorcerer's targeted recipients are susceptible to invasive magic and may sense danger, power, and the uncanny precisely at that juncture of body and lifeworld. From the sorcerer's perspective, bodily boundaries are porous (Kapferer 1997; Stewart and Strathern 2002:83–107).

Excursus: Cognitive Theories of "Belief" and Ritual

It would be a disservice not to mention cognitive science in this sketch, since cognitive science has claimed, extraordinarily, to have deduced organic bases for religious "belief" and for ritualization as a way of coping with intuited threats. Most of the cognitive theorists address very few of the ritual and ideational dynamics summarized earlier. Instead, they focus strikingly and controversially on what is called the hypersensitive agent detective device

---

[62] Stewart and Strathern have explored the dynamics of revenge from Montenegro to Sri Lanka to the Pacific Islands (2002:108–136).

(HADD) and the necessary "error management" of wrong interpretations of those agents (Barrett 2011, McCauley and Lawson 2002, Guthrie 2007). Striking for explaining ritual behavior is the conjunction of a "Hazard-Precaution System" based on existential anxiety with an "action parsing" system "concerned with the division of the flow of behavior into meaningful units" (Boyer and Liénard 2006:1), through which anxieties are assuaged (2006:7). Additionally, McCauley and Lawson propose culturally postulated superagents (CPS) (2002:8, 19) as constituent components of ritual behaviors. Curious readers will consult the forenamed sources, but following is a summary of the main points.

Cognitive science imputes "religion," which it defines as the ascription of agency to supernaturals, to natural features of humans as a species. For McCauley and Lawson, we are born over-prepared to detect superagency in our environments and detect it "far more liberally than stimuli demand" (2002:21). This lingering HADD is explained as an evolutionary offshoot of such days as we were predators and prey, when heightened perceptions would have boosted our likelihood of survival. As Guthrie mimes, we are still "on a hair trigger to detect friend or foe, predator or prey, we cannot prevent ourselves from thinking we have detected one even when none is there" (2007:52). Cognitivists adduce this tendency to impute agency, supernatural and otherwise, to a species-specific and "mostly unconscious search . . . for all possible agents in a perceptually ambiguous world" (Guthrie 2007:52).

Four rudimentary structures of the human mind are invoked to support the theory. First is the aforementioned predilection to attribute agency to moving objects, dangerous or not. Cognitivists hold that this is fully present in five-month-olds (Guthrie 2007:47–48). Although we learn to manage interpretive errors of perception (e.g., not every shadow is a predator), the imputation of agency to moving objects remains implicit. One gauge of this is that we keenly detect moving objects in our environments peripherally, from the edge of the retina, whereas the color and shape of those objects often go unnoticed (Guthrie 2007:46); evolutionary necessity (survival instincts) is said to explain this sensitivity to peripheral perceptions of motion. Second, and overlapping, is our tendency to anthropomorphize events and things. Eyes, faces, bilateralism, the up–down axis of bodies like ours: we are sensitized, even primed, to perceive these features in animals and things surrounding us, as cognitive studies show. Part of this anthropomorphism is attributing intentionality and goal-orientation to moving objects (Whitehouse 2007:259); in Guthrie's terms, we impute "minds behind events" (2007:48). This attribution of agency and anthropomorphism to events serves our navigation through a world full of possible dangers, but also helps to account for our persistent and intuitive discernment of causal superagents who look and behave much as we do (i.e., divinities). So does another construct, related to a theory of mind, called CAT, or cross-domain analogical thinking (Whitehouse 2007:261–273). Emergent with modern humans, CAT enabled us to analogize from our own nuclear experiences to global possibilities and to store enormous amounts of semantic memory. Evolutionarily, CAT greatly expanded what we could imagine, not only about cultural formations but about the cosmos surrounding us and of course about agents in that cosmos. A fourth rudimentary tendency, disputed by some (e.g., Guthrie 2007) but promoted by Boyer (2001:62), Barrett (2011) and others, is our tendency to fixate on counterintuitive notions. Counterintuitive notions arrest our attention because they mix ontologically intuitive categories with ones which defy ontology as we know it. One example is ghosts. According to these theorists, ghosts have bodies shaped like ours, bilateralism like ours, an up–down axis like ours, but they also have features which defy what is natural, e.g., transparency and the ability to penetrate walls and transcend death. The ghost is fascinating (a "salient cognitive gadget" [Boyer 2001:235]) because of its combination of human and nonhuman attributes. The same may be said of a god, who is like a person but with omniscience, or a zombie, who is like a person but without consciousness (Boyer 2001:63). All four of these rudimentary structures are said to support religion – defined as belief in supernatural causal agents – as an adaptive by-product of our evolution. By this theory, meaning per se notably is reduced to its cognitive foundations and evolutionary roots (McCauley and Lawson 2002:10–11, 105).

At its core, ritual too lacks semantic and cultural meaning, according to McCauley and Lawson (2002:9–11). Instead, ritualization is impelled by "impli-cit operations of a cognitive system geared to the handling of potentially hazardous materials in the environment" (Whitehouse 2007:253, paraphrasing Boyer and Liénhard 2006). Notwithstanding its utility for our ancestors, the continued compulsion to ritualization is likened by cognitivists to the pathology of obsessive compulsive disorder (OCD) (Boyer and Liénhard 2006:2–3), which arises from diffuse anxieties without rational source. For OCD sufferers, cognitive arousal may take the form of intrusive thoughts, fears of contamina-tion, foreboding about inflicting harm on others, etc., which are in effect mal-adaptations of the HADD. These fears tend to be managed psychologically by action parsing rituals, such as endlessly repeating behaviors which do not actually target the source of anxiety but do pacify that anxiety. Ancestrally the hazard-precaution mechanism would have been rooted in threats to survi-val, not only in threatening predators but in various contaminants (rotting meat, feces, infected wounds [Whitehouse 2007:255]); in today's experience, the hazard-precaution mechanism may be triggered by associated exposures which are not actually dangerous – for instance, exposures to substances which give rise to disgust but do not threaten life. Ritualized responses to both the original and the symbolic threat, say Boyer and Liénhard, are compulsive, rigid, lacking in rational goals, repetitious and redundant, and restricted in theme (2006:4). The difference between the ritualized responses of OCD sufferers and of participants in cultural rituals is a matter of degree. OCD sufferers tend to be caught in a feed-back loop; participants in cultural rituals are not so caught, but do tend to be motivated by a particular, unconscious urgency (Boyer 2001:237). For some cognitivists, such as McCauley and Lawson, religious rituals are distinguished by the felt presence of culturally postulated superagents, who are credited with bringing about a change in the world, and presumably with lessening this motivational urgency (2002:14). For others, such as Boyer, gods and spirits are unnecessary add-ons, but particularly salient when a ritual is expected to divert danger (2001:237).

How these theories relate to ritual and violence is basic. If ritualization and religion too are responses to a perception of danger, one would think that both are evolutionarily tied to anticipated or actual violence in the form of potential personal injury and/or risk to species survival. Within this scheme, one can imagine ritualization as a response to a perception of the uncanny, of evil, or the felt presence of extraordinary amoral powers. Restricting the understanding of ritual to an evolutionarily ingrained response to danger, one might see how an impulse to ritualization could be harnessed to assuage anxieties and, presumably also, collectively to bolster defense against danger, or at least to make an impressive show toward that end (as in apelike beatings of the chest). Presumably, these impressive shows would encourage social solidarity and hence serve functionalist ends. Yet, as hopefully this booklet has shown, this understanding of ritualization is simple, at best. Ritualization does not have to be reflexive and devoid of meaning. It does not have to be a response to danger, and it is certainly not always devoid of art.

As for the merits of the theories on their faces, it would be rash to deny any cognitive architecture to religion and ritual. But philosophers, anthropologists, and scholars of religion will observe just how much these cognitive theories omit and what hegemonic presumptions they bring to the discussion. A few critical points are summarized here.

From the start, there is the circularity deriving from the definition of religion as belief in supernatural, causal agents, a belief understood as a cognitive error in need of management. This restriction of religion to the category of belief – an apparent carryover from the Enlightenment – may engage the claims of mainstream Protestant Christianity and Islam, the world traditions most fixated on deistic metaphysical claims. But note that, first, these are very restrictive metaphysical claims even for those traditions, with their vast histories, social formations, and mystical offshoots – one need only think of Pentecostal pursuit of a ritualized apotheosis abetted by music (Becker 2004:97–99) or Sufi qawwali performances wherein dancing is hoped to become ecstatic and to merge the dancer with the divine. These coveted altered states clearly involve more than belief. Second, and relatedly, the confinement of religion to belief can hardly do justice to religious experiences of people involved in animistic and/or pantheistic traditions in all their diversity of adherence to the felt presence of powers and power-manifestations. As we have seen, ethnomusicologists offer much richer accounts of ritual and religious perceptions from the inside, including visceral visitations by spirits (especially Friedson [1996, 2009]). Metaphysical claims are quite irrelevant to, and barely even interesting for, grasping the full dynamism of experiences which tend to be rooted in the body. This is not to mention the irrelevance of deistic claims for world traditions which espouse no gods in the agentive sense conceived by cognitivists (e.g., Theravadan Buddhism and Jainism). The confinement of religion to belief therefore greatly restricts what may be covered under the domain of the cognitive science of religion.

Relatedly, cognitive theories embrace Western empirical presumptions about what measurably exists or not, and about the very nature of agents and objects. Existence is obviously relative to perception – some traditions clearly strive to cultivate altered or enhanced perceptions of what exists – and, as Stewart and Strathern point out, careful ethnography has disclosed quite different accounts of agency among various peoples (2014:109, 111, 114–116). For some aboriginal peoples the entire world is conceived as a living being descended from ancestral figures and dreamt by them. Presumably the separation between agents and perceived objects will be conceived quite differently in such a dream-world than they are by the terms of a Western three-dimensional reality. In any case, those Western terms of analysis would seem a hegemonic imposition on the enmeshed agent–object perceptions of animists. Superstition is the coinage once applied to perceptions which eluded Enlightenment frames of reference, and arguably it remains implicit in the cognitivist's take on religion.

Perhaps most importantly, as James Laidlaw points out (2007), religious and ritual traditions are vastly more than their evolutionary wellsprings. Not only are there histories and sociologies and psychologies of traditions; there are what we might here call aesthetic dimensions, not reducible to their cognitive systems. He provides the comparison to Donatello's David (2007:232). We can admit that understanding this David as a work of metallurgy is important for grasping the history of technology, but metallurgy is quite ancillary to grasping the statue as a work of art, as, indeed, the image of an effeminate boy who has intrigued viewers for centuries. The pleasing nature of the sculpture is not just about recognition of human features; Donatello has cast a specific interpretation of this biblical figure, the son of Jesse who was ruddy, handsome, with beautiful eyes, and appealing to Saul (initially), to Jonathan, and to Michal and all the women who sang of his accomplishments (all in 1 Samuel). Similarly to metallurgy, cognitive science can provide only the most rudimentary tools for gaining insight into figures like this. What it lacks (and Whitehouse acknowledges this lack [2007]) is an informed interpretation based on historical contingency. While there are certainly common developments in religious traditions, each development is most fully appreciated in the context of its particular historical exigencies and humanistic response to those exigencies, rather than as the fulfillment of cognitive predilections.

For Laidlaw, what the cognitive predilections cannot account for includes reason, imagination, and will, which might be re-parsed (by the present author) as consciousness and a range of creative, historically contingent, human choices. In a nutshell, whatever organic seeds may linger in our urge to see faces in the clouds and to perform dances to them, our poetic and artistic delight in spectacles and performances is polyvalent and historically fascinating, simply as a creative human product. The same may be said for ritual and religious experiences which give rise to and respond to terror. These exceed what cognitive theory can explain; hence, the robust literature on trauma, pain, and theodicy. Reductionist analysis is not the same thing as cogent analysis. Evolutionary kernels can account only for so much.

Section III: Rituals of Menace

With these expository rubrics in mind, let us now focus briefly on a category of ritual which communicates in a fairly transparent way and which has been touched upon in passing. We will call these rituals of menace – as in cursing and threatening rituals, with their staged displays. It is obvious that menacing rituals combine our principal interests of ritual and violence, even if the violence is only implied. We have already treated the different degrees of transparency in ritual dynamics; the example of the Kamajors has shown that not all rituals communicate menace straightforwardly. Those discussed in this section, though, do communicate in a fairly transparent way, at least on their faces. They illustrate some basic ritual dynamics and yet they are separated historically by millennia. They are ancient Near Eastern oath-swearing rituals and the Islamic State (IS) staged beheadings of 2014.

Despite the relatively straightforward nature of these extremely violent displays, readers would do well to remember the subtleties of ritual seduction and the ritual imaginary, as described earlier. Obviously both ritualizations occur in complex historical contexts which lie beyond the scope of this discussion and are possibly incapable of being entirely captured, given the constraints of our ancient evidence in particular. However, although some of their performative dynamics probably elude us, anyone with a body can grasp the most overt of those dynamics. Rituals of menace are intended to evoke a strong visceral response. Indeed, these are some of the most grisly rituals known to the present author. Harking back to our earlier discussion of ritualized communication, we can note that rituals of menace tend to be grasped somatically and iconically – or, in other terms, by the body and the eye. As argued earlier (relying on Csordas), somatic and iconic comprehensions are not necessarily distinct in experience. Following is a brief recapitulation of the dynamics.

The re-entry of the body into cultural analysis and aesthetics has been noted. On the one hand, privileging embodiment in any cultural analysis is still somewhat controversial. Since Foucault we have learned to distrust our immediate bodily perceptions, given the ostensible layers of cultural imposition on perceptions, if not the actual cultural construction of them. On the other hand, certain existential phenomenologists and ritualists controverted this distrust by embracing the philosophical notion of intentionality and by stressing the lived body as a source for meaning. Attending closely to the processes of somatic attention, Csordas described how shapes emerge from the broader horizon of awareness, before they become graspable as shapes (2002) – there is no clean break between the perceiving self and what is perceived. Then there is Bryan Turner's account of some meanings which tend to be anchored in bodily homologies (1992:107–112, 117–122). Pleasure and disgust tend to be measured by reference to the human face and body and, as noted in our discussion of cognitive science, recent theories suggest that we classify shapes and qualities by virtue of familiarity with ourselves (Guthrie 2007:46–48). Lakoff and Johnson argued that ethical notions, such as compassion and morality, were rooted in metaphoric ascriptions based on embodiment – health, strength, wealth, purity, control, nurturance, etc. (1999:331). Perhaps most fascinating to explore, though, are extreme pain and music. Both have been argued to engage us at a level deeper than discourse and to precipitate wordless bodily awarenesses, in some cases transformative awarenesses (Crapanzano 2004:84–93, Whitehouse 2004; Alcorta and Sosis 2013; Friedson 1996, 2009; Becker 2004). While these theories do not privilege the body in identical ways, embodiment would seem an inescapable point of reference for all of them. Embodied understanding is crucial for grasping the communicational dynamic behind rituals of menace.

Also argued earlier is that ritual understanding relies on pattern recognition and figural awareness, a combination which Tambiah identified as an iconic dimension of communication. On the one hand, recognizing the iconic is like perceiving an underlying shape in an abstract representation (e.g., perceiving familiar shapes and behaviors in the Loma masking rituals, described earlier). Pattern recognition is a learned recognition, and intrinsically cultural. On the other hand, relying on Langer and others, we pointed out that the ritual spectacle, like art, engages the eye organically, through the presentation of rhythms, tensions and resolutions (Langer 1951). Combining the two, we see that vision is both culturally encumbered and not. For Morgan, seeing is affected by powerful dispositions, which cast a light on and help to construct the realities that we see (2012:22–23, 33). On the cultural side, he discusses the powerful example of the shaming gaze (2012:6), but also notes that ways of seeing may be cultivated by religious praxis, as in fasting, meditating, yogic exercises, sweat lodges, and peyote. Seeing is an interface between body and world, a vehicle to touching, tracing, and beholding, and occurs in collaboration with the body (Morgan 2012:48). For our purposes, the haptic aspect of seeing is important: mapped onto the seen may be sensory features such as texture, touch, proximity, movement (Morgan 2012:111–126), and conceivably, too, a tactile grasp of someone else's susceptibility to pain: anyone who can see can experience these.

As we shall see, rituals of menace adjoin the iconic and the somatic in communicating a felt threat to one's being.

Ancient Oath-Making Spectacles

For our first example, let us consider ancient oath-cursing spectacles, as described in treaties and referred to earlier. Oath-cursing spectacles are one element within a whole genre of international diplomatic rituals extending from the ancient Near East into the Homeric epics, dating from the Near Eastern Middle Bronze Age into the first millennium BCE. Oath-curses conclude actual treaties, are reported in correspondence about treaties (particularly in complaints about perjury), and, in a world lacking international sanctions, obviously play an important role in inter-state as well as interpersonal relations. The weight of this role may be gauged by the cost of violation. Hence:

> This shoulder is not the shoulder of a spring lamb, it is the shoulder of Mati'ilu, it is the shoulder of his sons, his magnates, and the people of his land. If Mati'ilu should sin against this treaty, so may, just as the shoulder of this spring lamb is torn out ... the shoulder of Mati'ilu, of his sons, [his magnates] and the people of his land be torn out. (Arnold and Beyer 2002:101)

> [J]ust as [thi]s ewe has been cut open and the flesh of [her] young has been placed in her mouth, may they make you eat in your hunger the flesh of your brothers, your sons and your daughters. (Luckenbill 1968:52, section 69)

> Just as young sheep and ewes and male and female spring lambs
> are slit open and their entrails rolled down over their feet, so
> may (your entrails and) the entrails of your sons and your
> daughters roll down over your feet. (Parpola and Watanabe
> 1988, section 70)

While particularly vivid, these Assyrian examples are not different in kind from biblical and Homeric examples. Naturally, one cannot be certain whether oath-curses describe actual performances or just the imagination of them, but their plenitude in ancient textual evidence cannot be disputed.[63] Nor can some of their ritual dynamics.

Their most obvious common feature is staged cruelty. From ripping out the shoulders and slitting open the stomachs of victims, the cruelty is unmistakable. The fate of the sheep in the second example rivets attention and generates a specter not only of bodily mutilation, but also of cannibalism. It surely was expected also to generate a shudder of horror and a visceral repulsion to the spectacle, reflecting the consequences of perjury. These responses are based partly on a violent imaginary, to be sure – there are doubtlessly unsettling forces, explicit or inchoate, human or supernatural, anticipated to visit these punishments on perjurers.[64] But more immediately they rely on a tactile imagination of pain and a certain empathy whereby the viewer is at least fleetingly absorbed into the experience of the sheep.[65] Needless to say, comprehension of suffering and death relies on somatic understanding of what it means to be embodied and alive, as well as on a basic figural transference,

---

[63] See overviews by Hillers (2015:97–201), Weinfeld (1990:175-91), and, outstandingly, Kitz (2013).

[64] Kitts 2005, 2011, 2015.

[65] Morgan treats a similar absorption into the fetish of the sacred heart (2012: 111–136).

whereby the sheep's mutilation and cannibalism of kin is mapped onto the perceiver's own situation. The spectacle is personalized and visualized, in all its horror. It would be hard to deny that these displays are meant to remind one of one's own bodily fragility and to elicit a fearful specter of lethal force, similar to that imposed on the sheep.

IS Beheading Message Videos

IS beheading "message" videos of 2014 were sculpted to similar ends, way beyond whatever Ur-models they purported to invoke from hadith or Qur'an. As choreographed performances, these were easily viewed as rituals, and even as sworn oaths. Consider the Sotloff beheading video produced by IS in November 2014. While not beautiful in any traditional sense (to most of us), it was nonetheless costumed and choreographed for full theatrical effect[66] – staged in a featureless desert, the iconic IS flag flying in the upper left corner, the victim costumed in the familiar orange jumpsuit and executioner in the black robe, baklava, brown pistol holder, and brandished knife. The only sound was the wind and of course the victim's testimony and the executioner's promises to slaughter his enemies. These were traditional promises, matching at least two previous videos. Equally traditional were the executioner's staged neck-sawing motion and the camera fade-out. Within 20 seconds after we heard and watched the victim speak, we saw a video sweep from his feet up to his waist, which held the head that just spoke. The professional production quality to these videos has been discussed widely,[67] but one needn't boast a professional eye to grasp the startle-effect of

[66] www.military.com/daily-news/2014/09/02/video-purports-to-show-beheading-of-us-journalist.html

[67] See, e.g., "ISIS Hostage Videos: Are They Done Outside?" Military.com, at www.washingtonpost.com/world/national-security/inside-the-islamic-states-propa

viewing the severed head which just moments before was speaking. The spectacular dimension was inexorable.

The sensory effects were also inexorable. Not only were there the sound of the wind, the visual theatrics (costuming, weapons, flag) and the predictable sequence of events, but, as with the previous videos by the same executioner, the actual neck-sawing is barely suggested, just enough to conjure for spectators the tactile experience of being beheaded, like the victim. The fully staged spectacle riveted attention. Viewers were absorbed into the entire spectacle, which was amplified by ritualized gravitas, the slow and deliberate pacing, the obvious testifying quality to the speeches, explicit proclamations about future behaviors – no one could deny that the whole thing was meant to generate shock and awe. It was seemingly impossible not to be engaged with the spectacle, if one's eyes were open at all. To add to the experience was the obvious haptic dimension of grasping the tactile effects of the seen (Morgan's point), as well as the implicitly visual mapping of Sotloff's experience, namely his beheading, onto ourselves.

The Two Compared

Similarly to the oath-cursing ritual, the IS beheading video relied on corporeal and iconic dimensions of recognition – we recognized the pain and the pattern. But there is another obvious commonality. That is the oath – the executioner in the IS video explicitly testified to his intention to bring similar harm to his enemies, who would suffer a similar fate as his victim.[68] The oath-making ritual

ganda-machine/2015/11/20/051e997a-8ce6-11e5-acff-673ae92ddd2b_story.html? utm_term=.8548ac6e3ae8.

[68] Similarly, reputed IS leader, Al Bagdadi, boasted in the same month of oaths of allegiance from supporters in Saudi Arabia, Yemen, Egypt, Libya, and Algeria: www.thedailybeast.com/articles/2014/11/16/kassig-video-a-recruitment-tool-for-isis.htm.

from antiquity too promises the fate of the sheep to oath-violators. The theme is familiar. While not always as gruesome, oath-making rituals are utilized in conflicts world round to intensify commitments and to impose gravitas on missions and warriors alike.

Another feature common to these two rituals is, obviously, the dimension of ritualized cruelty – namely, the use of a living victim to demonstrate lethal intent. If these were rare rituals, we might assign them to rare sadistic tendencies, but they are not rare. They are as common as conflict and may be found in conflicts world round, although ancient oath-making performances have received more attention than contemporary ones. While these performances do not occur in historical and cultural vacuums, it is indisputable that rituals of menace communicate in a relatively transparent way. Both rituals rely for effect on the same somatic and iconic dynamics, and viewers get it intuitively. Rituals of menace rely on fundamental communicational dynamics which we grasp through the body and the eye.

Despite the transparent ritual dynamics, it is conceivable that ritualized cruelties in the ancient oath-sacrifices at some point failed to command attention, and that those of contemporary IS beheading videos similarly will fail. As discussed in Section I, there is always the possibility of spectacular abuse becoming kitsch, predictable, banal, in contemporary as well as ancient times. If ancient reports are to be trusted, oath-sacrifices did fail to intimidate some participants, who did violate the sworn oaths and risked a horrible demise. It is arguable that the IS propaganda videos too are already transitioning from Sontag's aesthetics of depravity (2003) to Giroux's depravity of aesthetics (2011), thus diminishing in impact for contemporary audiences, who increasingly are inured to spectacles of cruelty.

For most of us, however, such stagings of ritualized abuse still evoke a rapt gaze and visceral horror. Despite the multidimensionality of our responses, it would seem that spectacles of terror, trauma, and extreme pain still can disturb received cultural constructions and throw us back to a profound sense of the uncanny, of virtual contingency, and of the "potential rupture within our customary worlds" (Strathern and Stewart 2006:7). Because of the high register to these performances, the effect is amplified and likely will continue to arrest attention for anyone who can imagine and personalize the effects.

Works Cited

Afsaruddin, Asma. "Martyrdom and Its Contestations in the Formative Period of Islam." In *Martyrdom, Self-Sacrifice, and Self-Immolation: Religious Perspectives on Suicide*, ed. Margo Kitts. New York: Oxford University Press, 2018. 85–105.

Ahmed, Sara and Jackie Stacey. "Introduction: Dermographies." In *Thinking Through the Skin*, eds. Sara Ahmed and Jackie Stacey. London and New York: Routledge, 2001. 1–17.

Aijmer, Göran. "Introduction: The Idiom of Violence in Imagery and Discourse." In *Meanings of Violence: A Cross-Cultural Perspective*, eds. Göran Aijmer and Jon Abbink. Oxford: Berg, 2000. 1–54.

Alcorta, Candace and Richard Sosis, "Ritual, Emotion, and Sacred Symbols," *Human Nature* 16:4 (2005): 323–359.

   "Ritual, Religion, and Violence: An Evolutionary Perspective." In *Oxford Handbook of Religion and Violence*, eds. Mark Juergensmeyer, Margo Kitts, and Michael Jerryson. New York: Oxford University Press, 2013. 571–596.

Alexander, Jeffrey C., "From the Depths of Despair: Performance, Counterperformance and 'September 11,'" *Sociological Theory* 22:1 (Mar. 2004): 88–104.

Allen, Mark W. and Elizabeth N. Arkush. "Introduction: Archaeology and the Study of War." In *The Archaeology of Warfare: Prehistories of Raiding and Conquest*. Gainesville: University of Florida Press, 2006, 1–22.

Archi, Alfonso. "Il Culto Del Focolare presso gli Ittiti." *SMEA* XVI (1975): 77–87.

Arnold, Bill T. and E. Bryan, eds. *Readings from the Ancient Near East: Primary Sources for Old Testament Study*. Grand Rapids: Baker Academic Press, 2002.

Works Cited

Asad, Talal. "Toward a Genealogy of the Concept of Ritual." *Genealogies of Religion*. Baltimore. The Johns Hopkins University Press 1993, 55–62, 307. In *Ritual*, eds. Pamela Stewart and Andrew Strathern. Farnham: Ashgate Press. 2010, 233–242.

Atkin, Albert, "Peirce's Theory of Signs", *The Stanford Encyclopedia of Philosophy* (Summer 2013 edition), ed.Edward N. Zalta, http://plato.stanford.edu/archives/sum2013/entries/peirce-semiotics/.

Austin, J. L. *How to Do Things with Words*. Cambridge, MA: Harvard University Press, 1962, 1975.

Bahn, Paul G. *Cambridge Illustrated History of Prehistoric Art*. Cambridge: Cambridge University Press, 1998.

Bahrani, Zainab. *The Graven Image*. Philadelphia: University of Pennsylvania Press, 2003.

"The King's Head." *Iraq* LXVI (2004): 115–118.

Rituals of War. New York: Zone Books, 2008.

Bar-Yosef, Ofer. "The Upper Paleolithic Revolution." *Annual Review of Anthropology* 31 (2002):363–393.

Bargu, Banu. *Starve and Immolate: The Politics of Human Weapons*. New York: Columbia University Press, 2014.

Barrett, Justin. *Cognitive Science, Religion, and Theology: From Human Minds to Divine Minds*. Conshohocken: Templeton Press, 2011.

Bateson, Gregory. *Steps to an Ecology of Mind*. New York: Ballantine Books, 1972.

Baudrillard, Jean. *The Spirit of Terrorism*. Trans. Chris Turner. London: Verso, 2002.

Becker, Judith O. *Deep Listeners: Music, Emotion, and Trancing*. Bloomington: Indiana University Press, 2004.

Beidelman, Thomas O. *The Cool Knife: Imagery of Gender, Sexuality, and Moral Education in Kaguru Initiation Ritual*. Ann Arbor: Smithsonian Institution Press, 1997.

Works Cited

Bell, Catherine. *Ritual Theory, Ritual Practice*. New York: Oxford University Press, 1992.

    "Ritual Symbols, Syntax, and Praxis: Questions of Cultural Meaning and Interpretation." In *Ritual: Perspectives and Dimensions*. New York: Oxford University Press (1997), 61–83, 281–285, 313–315. In *Ritual*, eds. Pamela Stewart and Andrew Strathern. Farnham: Ashgate Press. 2010. 21–52.

Bell, Vikki. "The Scenography of Suicide: Terror, Politics, and the Humiliated Witness." *Economy and Society* 34/2 (2005):241–260.

Benjamin, Walter. "Critique of Violence." In *Reflections: Essays, Aporisms, Autobiographical Writings*. Trans. Edmund Jephcott. New York: Schocken Books. 1986 (1921). 277–300.

Benn, James A. *Burning for the Buddha*. Honolulu: University of Hawai'i Press, 2007.

Binder, Werner. "Ritual Dynamics and Torture: The Performance of Violence and Humiliation at the Abu Ghraib Prison." *Ritual Dynamics and the Science of Ritual*, Volume III: State, Power, and Violence, eds. Margo Kitts, Bernd Schneidmüller, Gerald Schwedler, Eleni Tounta, Hermann Kulke, and Uwe Skoda. Wiesbaden: Harrassowitz, 2010. 75–104.

Bloch, Maurice. "Symbols, Song, Dance and Features of Articulation: Is Religion an Extreme Form of Traditional Authority?" *Archives Europeenes de Sociologie* 15 (1974):55–81.

    Political Language and Oratory in Traditional Society. London: Academy Press, 1975.

    Prey into Hunter. Cambridge: Cambridge University Press, 1992.

    "Ritual and Deference." In *Ritual and Memory: Toward a Comparative Anthropology of Religion*, eds. Harvey Whitehouse and James Laidlaw. Lanham: Rowman and Littlefield 2004. 65–78.

Works Cited

"Symbols, Song, Dance and Features of Articulation: Is Religion an Extreme Form of Traditional Authority?" In *Ritual, History and Power: Selected Papers in Anthropology*. London: Athlone Press. 19–45, 214, 223–224, 1989. Excerpted in *Ritual*, eds. Pamela Stewart and Andrew Strathern. Farnham: Ashgate Press. 2010. 53–82.

Bobič, Pavlina. *War and Faith: The Catholic Church in Slovenia, 1914–1918*. Leiden; Boston: Brill, 2012.

Bottéro, Jean. *Religion in Mesopotamia*. Trans. Teresa Lavender Fagan. Chicago: University of Chicago Press, 2001.

Bourdieu, Pierre. *Outline of a Theory of Practice*. Cambridge: Cambridge University Press, 1977.

Boyer, Pascal. *Religion Explained: The Evolutionary Origins of Religious Thought*. New York: Basic Books, 2001.

Boyer, Pascal and Pierre Liénhard. "Why Ritualized Behavior? Precaution Systems and Action Parsing in Developmental, Pathological, and Cultural Rituals." *Behavioral and Brain Sciences* 29 (2006):1–56.

Burkert, Walter. *Homo Necans: The Anthropology of Ancient Greek Sacrificial Ritual and Myth*. Trans. Peter Bing. Berkeley and Los Angeles: University of California Press, 1983.

"Sacrificial Violence: A Problem in Ancient Religions." In *Oxford Handbook of Religion and Violence*, eds. Mark Juergensmeyer, Margo Kitts, and Michael Jerryson. New York: Oxford University Press, 2013. 437–453.

Castelli, Elizabeth A. *Martyrdom and Memory: Early Christian Culture Making*. New York: Columbia University Press, 2004.

Chacon, Richard and David Dye, eds. *The Taking and Displaying of Human Body Parts as Trophies by Amerindians*. New York: Springer-Verlag, 2007.

Chacon, Richard and Ruben Mendoza, eds. *North American Indigenous Warfare and Ritual Violence*. Tucson: University of Arizona Press, 2007.

Works Cited

Chagnon, Napoleon A. "Life Histories, Blood Revenge, and Warfare in a Tribal Population." *Science*, New Series 239:4843 (Feb. 26, 1988): 985–992.

Chippindale, Christopher. "Current Issues in the Study of Palaeolithic Images." *American Journal of Archaeology* 103/1 (Jan.1999):113–117.

Collon, Dominique. "Dance in Ancient Mesopotamia." *Near Eastern Archaeology* 66/3 (2003): 96–102.

Conkey, Margaret W. "New Approaches in the Search for Meaning? A Review of Research in Paleolithic Art." *Journal of Field Archaeology* 14/4 (Winter 1987):413–430.

Cook, David. "Martyrdom Operations in Contemporary Jihad Literature." *Novo Religio* 6/1 (2002): 7–44.

    Understanding Jihad. Oakland: University of California Press, 2005.

    Martyrdom in Islam. Cambridge: Cambridge University Press, 2007.

    Princeton Readings in Religion and Violence. "9/11 Conspirator. Last Instructions." [Trans. David Cook, from the Arabic version published in the New York Times.] In *Princeton Readings in Religion and Violence*, eds Mark Juergensmeyer and Margo Kitts. Princeton: Princeton University Press, 2011. 83–39.

Crane, Susan A. "Choosing Not to Look: Representation, Repatriation, and Holocaust Atrocity Photography." *History and Theory* 47 (October 2008):309–330.

Crapanzano, Vincent. *Imaginative Horizons: An Essay in Literary-Philosophical Anthropology.* Chicago: University of Chicago Press, 2004.

Csordas, Thomas J. "Embodiment as a Paradigm for Anthropology." *Ethos* 18/1 (1990):5–47.

    "The Rhetoric of Transformation in Ritual Healing," in *Body/Meaning/Healing.* New York: Palgrave, 2002. 11–57.

deBoeck, Filip. "The Apocalyptic Interlude: Revealing Death in Kinshasa." *African Studies Review* 48/2 (2005):11–32.

Works Cited

Dissanayake, Ellen. "An Ethological Review of Human Ritual and Art in Evolutionary History." *Leonardo* 12 (1979):27–31.

"Ritual and Ritualization: Musical Means of Conveying and Shaping Emotion in Humans and Other Animals," in *Music and Manipulation: On the Social Uses and Social Control of Music*, eds. Steven Brown and Ulrich Voglsten. Oxford and New York: Berghahn Books, 2006. 31–56. Available online at https://ellendissanayake.com/publications/pdf/RitualAndRitualization_EllenDissanayake%20.pdf (accessed November 27, 2017).

Durkheim, Émile. *The Elementary Forms of Religious Life*. Trans. Carol Cosman. Oxford: Oxford University Press, 2001.

Eco, Umberto. *On Ugliness*. New York: Rizzoli, 2007.

Eidinow, Esther. *Oracles, Curses, and Risk among the Ancient Greeks*. New York: Oxford University Press, 2007/2010. doi: 10.1093/acprof: oso/9780199277780.001.0001

Ellis, Stephen. "Liberia 1989–1994: A Study of Ethnic and Spiritual Violence." *African Affairs* 94/375 (1995):165–197.

Escheverría Rey, Fernando. "Weapons, Technological Determinism, and Ancient Warfare." In *New Perspectives on Ancient Warfare*, eds. Garrett G. Fagan and Matthew Trundle. Boston: Brill, 2010. 21–56.

Evans-Pritchard, E.E. *Theories of Primitive Religion*. Oxford: Clarendon Press, 1965.

Ferguson, R. Brian. "'War Before Civilization: The Myth of the Peaceful Savage,' by Lawrence Keeley," (book review). *American Anthropologist* 99/2 (1997):424–425.

"Archaeology, Cultural Anthropology, and the Origins and Intensifications of War." In *The Archaeology of Warfare: Prehistories of Raiding and Conquest*, eds. Elizabeth N. Arkush and Mark W. Allen. Gainsville: University of Florida Press, 2006. 469–523.

"War before History." *The Ancient World at War*, ed. Philip de Souza. New York: Thames and Hudson, 2008. 15–27.

Ferme, Mariane C. *The Underneath of Things: Violence, History, and the Everyday in Sierra Leone*. Berkeley and Los Angeles: University of California Press, 2001.

Fernandez, James W. "The Performance of Ritual Metaphors." In *The Social Use of Metaphor*, eds. J. David Sapir and J. Christopher Crocker. Philadelphia: University of Pennsylvania Press (1977) 100–131.

"Persuasions and Performances: Of the Beast in Every Body ... And the Metaphors of Everyman." *Daedalus* 101/1 (1972):39–59.

Fierke, K. M. *Political Self-Sacrifice: Agency, Body and Emotion in International Relations*. New York: Cambridge University Press, 2013.

Foucault, Michel. *Discipline and Punish: The Birth of the Prison*. New York: Penguin Books, 1977.

Fouda, Yosri and Nick Fielding. *Masterminds of Terror: The Truth behind the Most Devastating Terrorist Attack the World Has Ever Seen*. Edinburgh: Main Stream Press, 2003.

Frazer, Sir James George. *The Golden Bough: A Study of Magic and Religion*. New York: MacMillan, 1951 (1922).

Freud, Sigmund. "The Uncanny." *Imago*. Trans. James Strachey and Anna Freud. In *The Standard Edition of the Complete Works of Sigmund Freud. Vol XVII. An Infantile Neurosis and Other Works*. London: Hogarth Press, *1917-1919*. 1919. Accessed March 14, 2015: https://uncanny.la.utexas.edu/wp-content/uploads/2016/04/freud-uncanny_001.pdf.

Totem and Taboo. Trans. A.A. Brills. New York: Vintage Books, 1946.

Friedson, Steven M. *Dancing Prophets: Musical Experience in Tumbuka Healing*. Chicago: University of Chicago Press, 1996.

Remains of Ritual: Northern Gods in a Southern Land. Chicago: University of Chicago Press, 2009.

Works Cited

Fuentes, Agustín. "It's Not All Sex and Violence: Integrated Anthropology and the Role of Cooperation and Social Complexity in Human Evolution." *American Anthropologist*, New Series, 106/4 (Dec. 2004):710–718.

"A New Synthesis: Resituating Approaches to the Evolution of Human Behavior." *Anthropology Today* 25/3 (2009):12–17

Geertz, Clifford. *The Interpretation of Cultures*. New York: Basic Books. 1973.

Geller, Stephen A. "The Prophetic Roots of Religious Violence in Western Religions." In *Religion and Violence: The Biblical Heritage*, eds. David A. Bernat and Jonathan Klawans. Sheffield: Sheffield Phoenix Press, 2007. 47–56.

Geschiere, Peter. "Witchcraft, Shamanism, and Nostalgia: A Review Essay." *Comparative Studies in Society and History* 58/1 (2016):242–265.

Giesen, Bernhard, and Daniel Šuber, *Religion and Politics: Cultural Perspectives*. Leiden: Brill 2005.

Girard, René. *Violence and the Sacred*. Trans. Patrick Gregory. Baltimore: Johns Hopkins University Press, 1977.

Things Hidden Since the Foundation of the World. Trans. Stephen Bann and Michael Metteer. Palo Alto: Stanford University Press, 1987.

Studies in Violence, Mimesis, and Culture: One by Whom Scandal Comes. Trans. M. B. DeBevoise. East Lansing: Michigan State University Press. 2014a.

Studies in Violence, Mimesis, and Culture: When These Things Begin: Conversations with Michel Treguer. Trans. Trevor Cribben Merrill. East Lansing: Michigan State University Press. 2014b.

Giroux, Henry A. "'Instants of Truth': The 'Kill Team' Photos and the Depravity of Aesthetics." *Afterimage* 39/1–2 (July 1, 2011). Accessed November 27, 2017: http://vsw.org/afterimage/issues/afterimage-vol-39-no-1-2/.

"Disturbing Pleasures." *Third Text* 26/3 (2012):259–273. Accessed November 27, 2017: http://www.tandfonline.com/doi/full/10.1080/09528822.2012.679036.

Glucklich, Ariel. *Sacred Pain: Hurting the Body for the Sake of the Soul.* New York: Oxford University Press, 2003.

Goffman, Erving. "Interaction Ritual: Deference and Demeanor." *Interaction Ritual: Essays on Face-to-Face Behavior*, 53–67, 77–81, 85–91 (1967). Reprinted in *Readings in Ritual Studies*, ed. Ronald L. Grimes. Upper Saddle River: Prentice Hall, 1996. 268–278.

Green, Alberto. *The Storm-God in the Ancient Near East.* Winona Lake: Eisenbrauns, 2003.

Grimes, Ronald L. "Ritual Criticism and Infelicitous Performances." In *Ritual Criticism: Case Studies in Its Practice, Essays on Its Theory*. University of South Carolina Press, 1990. Reprinted in *Readings in Ritual Studies*, ed. Ronald L. Grimes. Upper Saddle River: Prentice Hall, 1996. 279–292.

Guthrie, Stewart Elliot. "Anthropology and Anthropomorphism in Religion." In *Religion, Anthropology and Cognitive Science*, eds. Harvey Whitehouse and James Laidlaw. Durham: Carolina Academic Press 2007. 37–62.

Hafez, Mohammed. "Apologia for Suicide: Martyrdom in Contemporary Jihadist Discourse." In *Martyrdom, Self-Sacrifice, and Self-Immolation: Religious Perspectives on Suicide*, ed. Margo Kitts. New York: Oxford University Press, 2018. 126–139.

Handelman, Don. "Framing." *Theorizing Rituals, Vol. 1*, eds. Jens Kreinath, J. A. M. Snoek, and Michael Stausberg. Leiden: Brill, 2005. 571–582.

Handelman, Don and Galina Lindquist, eds. *Ritual in its Own Right.* New York: Berghahn Books, 2004.

Haraway, Donna. "Encounters with Companion Species: Entangling Dogs, Baboons, Philosophers, and Biologists." *Configurations* 14/1–2 (2006):97–114. https://doi.org/10.1353/con.0.0002.

Works Cited

Heidegger, Martin. *Being and Time.* Trans. John Macquarie and Edward Robinson. New York: Harper&Row, 1962.

Hillers, Delbert R. "Traditions in Treaty and Covenant." In *Poets Before Homer*, ed. F.W. Dobbs-Allsopp. Winona Lake: Eisenbrauns 2015. 97–201.

Højbjerg, Christian Kordt. "Masked Violence: Ritual Action and the Perception of Violence in an Upper Guinea Ethnic Conflict." In *Religion and African Civil Wars*, ed. Niels Kastfelt. New York: Palgrave MacMillan, 2005. 147–171.

    Resisting State Iconoclasm among the Loma of Guinea. Durham: Carolina Academic Press, 2007.

Holloway, Steven W. *Assur is King! Assur is King! Religion in the Exercise of Power in the Neo-Asyurian Empire.* Leiden: Brill, 2001.

Hughes, Dennis. *Human Sacrifice in Ancient Greece.* London: Routledge, 1991.

Huizinga, Johan. *Homo Ludens, A Study of the Play-Element in Culture.* Boston: Beacon Press, 1950.

Hutchinson, John. "Warfare and the Sacralisation of Nations: The Meanings, Rituals, and Politics of Remembrance." *Millennium: Journal of International Studies* 38/2 (2009):401–417.

Innis, Robert E. "The Tacit Logic of Ritual Embodiments: Rappaport and Polanyi between Thick and Thin." In *Ritual in its Own Right*, eds. Don Handelman and Galina Lindquist. New York: Berghahn Books, 2005. 197–212.

Insoll, Timothy. "The Archaeology of Religion and Rituals in Africa." In *The Oxford Handbook of African Archaeology*, eds. Peter Mitchell and Paul J. Lane. 2013. doi: 10.1093/oxfordhb/9780199569885.013.0012

Jensen, Adolf E. *Myth and Cult among Primitive Peoples.* Trans. M. T. Choldin and W. Weissleder. Chicago: University of Chicago Press, 1963.

Johnson, Mark. *The Body in the Mind.* Chicago: University of Chicago Press, 1987.

The Meaning of the Body. Chicago: University of Chicago Press, 2007.

Juergensmeyer, Mark. *Terror in the Mind of God*. Berkeley: University of California Press, 2000 (later editions: 2003, 2017).

"Religious Terrorism as Performance Violence." In *Oxford Handbook of Religion and Violence*, eds. Mark Juergensmeyer, Margo Kitts, and Michael Jerryson. New York: Oxford University Press, 2013. 280–292.

Juergensmeyer, Mark and Margo Kitts, eds. *Princeton Readings in Religion and Violence*. Princeton: Princeton University Press, 2011.

Juergensmeyer, Mark and Mona Kanwal Sheikh. "A Sociotheological Approach to Understanding Religious Violence." In *Oxford Handbook of Religion and Violence*, eds. Mark Juergensmeyer, Margo Kitts, and Michael Jerryson. New York: Oxford University Press. 620–644.

Kalleres, Dayna S. "The City in Late Antiquity: Where Have All the Demons Gone?" In *City of Demons*. Berkeley: University of California Press, 2014. doi:10.1525/california/9780520276475.003.0008

Kapferer, Bruce. *The Feast of the Sorcerer: Practices of Consciousness and Power*. Chicago: University of Chicago Press, 1997.

"Ritual Dynamics and Virtual Practice: Beyond Representation and Meaning." In *Ritual in its Own Right*, eds. Don Handelman and Galina Lindquist. New York: Berghahn Books. 2005. 35–54.

Keeley, Lawrence. *War Before Civilization*. New York: Oxford University Press, 1996.

Kelly, Raymond C. *Warless Societies and the Origin of War*. Ann Arbor: University of Michigan Press, 2000.

Kertzer, David I. "Ritual, Politics, and Power," [from *Ritual, Politics, and Power*, New Haven: Yale University Press, 1988, pp. 1–14, 92–101, and notes]. Excerpted in *Readings in Ritual Studies*, ed. Ronald L. Grimes. Upper Saddle River: Prentice Hall, 1996. 335–352.

Keyes Roper, Marilyn, "A Survey of the Evidence for Intrahuman Killing in the Pleistocene." *Current Anthropology* 10/4/2 (Oct., 1969):427–459.

Khosronejad, Pedram. "Introduction: Unburied Memories." *Visual Anthropology* 25 (2012):1–21.

Kippenberg, Hans. "'Consider That It Is a Raid on the Path of God': The Spiritual Manual of the Attackers of 9/11." *Numen* 52/1 (2005):29–58.

Kippenberg, Hans G. and Tilman Seidensticker, eds. *The 9/11 Handbook*. London: Equinox 2006.

Kitts, Margo. "Sacrificial Violence in the Iliad," *Journal of Ritual Studies* 16 (2002): 19–39.

    Sanctified Violence in Homeric Society. New York: Cambridge University Press, 2005/2012.

    "The Last Night: Ritualized Violence and the Last Instructions of 9/11." *Journal of Religion* 90/3 (2010a):283–312.

    "*Poinē* as a ritual leitmotif in the Iliad." In Vol. 3 of *Ritual Dynamics and the Science of Ritual*, eds. Margo Kitts, Bernd Schneidmüller, Gerald Schwedler, Eleni Tounta, Hermann Kulke, and Uwe Skoda. Wiesbaden: Harrassowitz, 2010b. 7–32.

    "Ritual scenes in the Iliad: rote, hallowed, or encrypted as ancient art?" *Oral Traditions* 26 (2011):1. http://journal.oraltradition.org/issues/26i/kitts.

    "Literary Approaches to Religion and Violence." In *Oxford Handbook of Religion and Violence*, eds. Mark Juergensmeyer, Margo Kitts, and Michael Jerryson. New York: Oxford University Press 2013a. 410–423.

    "The Near Eastern Chaoskampf in the River-Battle of Iliad 21." *Journal of Ancient Near Eastern Religions* 13/1 (2013b):86–112.

    "Anthropology and the Iliad." *Ashgate Research Companion to Anthropology*, eds Pamela Stewart and Andrew Strathern. Farnham: Ashgate Press, 2015. 389–410.

"Mimetic Rivalry, Sacrifice, and the Iliad?" *Bulletin for the Study of Religion* 45/3 (2016). doi: 10.1558/bsor.v45i3-4.31345.

"Discursive, Somatic, and Iconic Perspectives on Ritual." *Journal of Ritual Studies* 31/1 (2017a): 11–26.

"Ancient Near Eastern Perspectives on Evil and Terror." In *Cambridge Companion to the Problem of Evil*, eds. Chad Meister and Paul Moser. New York: Cambridge University Press, 2017b. 165–192.

ed. *Martyrdom, Self-Sacrifice, and Self-Immolation: Religious Perspectives on Suicide*, New York: Oxford University Press, 2018.

Kitts, Margo and Susumu Shimazono. "Rituals of Death and Remembrance." In *Oxford Handbook of Religion and Violence*, eds. Mark Juergensmeyer, Margo Kitts, and Michael Jerryson. New York: Oxford University Press, 2013. 345–350.

Kitz, Annemarie. *Cursed Are You!: The Phenomenology of Cursing in Cuneiform and Hebrew Texts*. Winona Lake: Eisenbrauns, 2013.

Knauft, Bruce M., Thomas S. Abler, Laura Betzig, Christopher Boehm, Robert Knox Dentan, Thomas M. Kiefer, Keith F. Otterbein, John Paddock, and Lars Rodseth. "Violence and Sociality in Human Evolution [and Comments and Replies]." *Current Anthropology* 32/4 (1991):391–428.

Laidlaw, James. "A Well-Disposed Social Anthropologists Problems with the 'Cognitive Science of Religion.'" In *Religion, Anthropology, and Cognitive Science*, eds. Harvey Whitehouse and James Laidlaw. Durham: Carolina Academic Press, 2007. 211–246.

Laidlaw, James and Harvey Whitehouse. "Introduction." In *Religion, Anthropology, and Cognitive Science*, eds. Harvey Whitehouse and James Laidlaw. Durham: Carolina Academic Press, 2007. 3–36.

Lakoff, George and Mark Johnson. *Metaphors We Live By*. Chicago: University of Chicago Press, 1980.

Philosophy in the Flesh. Chicago: University of Chicago Press, 1999.

Works Cited

Langer, Susanne. *Philosophy in a New Key*. New York: New American Library, 1951.

Levinson, Jon. *The Death and Resurrection of the Beloved Son*. New Haven: Yale University Press, 1993.

Luckenbill, Daniel David. *Ancient Records of Assyria and Babylonia, Vols. I* and *II* (originally published 1927, Chicago: University of Chicago, 1927, 1928 [2 vols.]) New York: Greenwood Press, 1968.

Mack, Burton. 1987. "Introduction: Religion and Ritual." In *Violent Origins. Walter Burkert, René Girard, and Jonathan Z. Smith on Ritual Killing and Cultural Formation*, ed. Robertson G. Hamerton-Kelly, 1–70. Palo Alto: Stanford University Press.

Malkki, Liisa. *Purity and Exile: Violence, Memory, and National Cosmology among Hutu Refugees in Tanzania*. Chicago: University of Chicago Press, 1995.

Mauss, Marcel. "Techniques of the Body." In *Sociologie et Anthropologie*, 4th edn. Paris: Universitaires de France, 1968. 364–389.

McCauley, Robert E. and E. Thomas Lawson. *Bringing Ritual to Mind: Psychological Foundations of Cultural Forms*. Cambridge: Cambridge University Press, 2002.

Meade, Margaret. "Warfare is only an invention – not a biological necessity." *ASIA*, XL (1940). Downloaded from www.ppu.org.uk/learn/infodocs/st_invention.html.

Mbembé, Steven Randall J.-A. "African Modes of Self-Writing." *Public Culture* 14/1 (2002):239–273. doi:http://dx.doi.org/10.1215/08992363-14-1-239.

Merleau-Ponty, Maurice. *Phenomenology of Perception*. Trans. Colin Smith. London: Routledge and Kegan Paul, 1962.

Michaels, Axel. "Ritual and Meaning." In *Theorizing Rituals, Vol.1*, eds. Jan Snoek, Michael Stausberg, and Jens Kreinath. Leiden: Brill, 2006. 247–265

Michelsen, Nicholas. "The Political Subject of Self-Immolation." *Globalizations* 12/1 (2015):83–100. doi: 10.1080/14747731.2014.971540

Minford, John and Joseph S. M. Lau, eds. *Classical Chinese Literature: An Anthology of Translations, Volume 1: From Antiquity to the Tang Dynasty*. New York: Columbia University Press, 2000.

Morgan, David. *The Embodied Eye, Religious Visual Culture and the Social Life of Seeing*. Berkeley: University of California Press, 2012.

Morinis, Alan. "The Ritual Experience: Pain and the Transformation of Consciousness in Ordeals of Initiation." *Ethos* 13/2 (Summer 1985):150–174.

Moss, Candida. "The Martyr as Alter Christus." In *The Other Christs: Imitating Jesus in Ancient Near Eastern Ideologies of Martyrdom*. New York: Oxford University Press, 2010. 45–74.

Nash, George. "Assessing Rank and Warfare-strategy in Prehistoric Hunter-gatherer Society: A Study of Representational Warrior Figures in Rock-art from the Spanish Levant, Southeastern Spain." In *Warfare, Violence, and Slavery in Prehistory*, ed. Michael Parker Pearson. Oxford: British Archaeological Reports (December 31, 2005). 75–86.

Niditch, Susan. *War in the Hebrew Bible*. New York: Oxford University Press, 1993.

Noegel, Scott B. "Dismemberment, Creation, and Ritual: Images of Divine Violence in the Ancient Near East." In *Belief and Bloodshed*, ed. James K. Wellman, Jr. Lanham: Rowman and Littlefield Publishers, Inc., 2007. 13–28.

"The Ritual Use of Linguistic and Textual Violence in the Hebrew Bible and Ancient Near East." In *State, Power, and Violence. Vol. 3 of Ritual Dynamics and the Science of Ritual*, eds. Margo Kitts, Bernd Schneidmüller, Gerald Schwedler, Eleni Tounta, Hermann Kulke, and Uwe Skoda. Weisbaden: Harrassowitz, 2010. 33–46.

"Corpses, Cannibals, and Commensality.: A Literary and Artistic Shaming Convention in the Ancient Near East." *Journal of Religion and Violence* 4/3 (2016): 255–303.

Works Cited

Ohnuma, Reiko. "To Extract the Essence from this Essenceless Body: Self-Sacrifice and Self-Immolation in Indian Buddhism." In *Martyrdom, Self-Sacrifice, and Self-Immolation: Religious Perspectives on Suicide*, ed. Margo Kitts. New York: Oxford University Press, 2018. 241–265.

Olyan, Saul M. "Jehoiakim's Dehumanizing Interment as a Ritual Act of Reclassification," *Journal of Biblical Literature* 133/2 (2014):271–279.

  "The Instrumental Dimensions of Ritual Violence against Corpses in Biblical Texts." In *Ritual Violence in the Hebrew Bible: New Perspectives*, ed. Saul M. Olyan. New York: Oxford University Press, 2016. doi:10.1093/acprof:oso/9780190249588.003.0007

Otto, Rudolf. *The Idea of the Holy*. Trans. John W. Harvey. London: Oxford University Press, 1958.

Parpola, Simo, and Kazuko Watanbe, eds. *State Archives of Assyria, Vol. II, Neo-Assyrian Treaties and Loyalty Oaths*. Helsinki: The Neo-Assyrian Text Corpus Project and the Helsinki Press, 1988.

Partow, Negar. "Martyrdom and Legacy of Blood: A Case Study in Iran." *Contemporary Review of the Middle East*.1/2 (2014):165–188.

Perkins, Judith. *The Suffering Self: Pain and Narrative Representation in the Early Christian Era*. London: Routledge, 2002.

Puett, Michael. Ritual and the Subjunctive." In *Ritual and its Consequences: An Essay on the Limits of Sincerity*, eds. Adam B. Seligman, Robert P. Weller, and Simon Bennett. New York: Oxford University Press, 2008. 17–42.

Rappaport, Roy A. *Ritual and Religion in the Making of Humanity*. Cambridge: Cambridge University Press, 1999.

Rapport, Nigel. "'Criminals by Instinct': On the 'Tragedy' of Social Structure and the 'Violence' of Individual Creativity." In *Meanings of Violence: A Cross-Cultural Perspective*, eds. Göran Aimer and Jon Abbink, Oxford: Berg 2000. 39–54.

Works Cited

Richards, Paul. "The Emotions at War: A Musicological Approach to Understanding Atrocity in Sierra Leone." In *Public Emotions*, eds Perri 6 [*sic*], S. Radstone, C. Squire, and A. Treacher. Basingstoke: Palgrave, 2007. 62–84.

"Dressed to Kill: Clothing as Technology of the Body in the Civil War in Sierra Leone." *Journal of Material Culture* 14 (2009):495–512.

Ricoeur, Paul. "The Model of Text: Meaningful Action Considered as a Text." *New Literary History* 5/1 (1973):91–117.

"The Metaphorical Process as Cognition, Imagination, and Feeling." In *Philosophical Perspectives on Metaphor*, ed. Mark Johnson. University of Minnesota Press, 1981. 228–47.

Riley-Smith, Jonathan. "The State of Mind of Crusaders to the East, 1095–1300." *The Oxford Illustrated History of the Crusades*, ed. Jonathan Riley-Smith. New York: Oxford University Press, 1997. 66–90.

Robertson Smith, W. *The Religion of the Semites*. New York: Meridian Books (Burnett Lectures 1888–1889), 1957.

"Lectures on the Religion of the Semites" (Edinburgh: Black 1889), excerpted in *The Myth and Ritual Theory*, ed. Robert A. Segal. Malden: Blackwell Publishers, Inc. 1998. 17–34.

Scarry, Elaine. *The Body in Pain*. New York: Oxford University Press, 1987.

Schalk, Peter. "Memorialization of Martyrs in the Tamil Resistance Movement of Ilam/Lamka." In *State, Power, and Violence*, eds. Margo Kitts, Bernd Schneidmüller, Gerald Schwedler, Eleni Tounta, Hermann Kulke, and Uwe Skoda. Wiesbaden: Harrassowitz 2010. 55–74.

Schildkrout, Enid. "Inscribing the Body." *Annual Review of Anthropology* 33 (2004):319–344.

Schwemer, Daniel. "The Storm God of the Ancient Near East, Part I," *Journal of Ancient Near Eastern Religions* 7/2 (2007):121–168.

Works Cited

"The Storm God of the Ancient Near East, Part II," *Journal of Ancient Near Eastern Religions* 8/1 (2008): 1–44.

Schmidt, Bettina E. and Ingo Schröeder, eds. *Anthropology of Violence and Conflict*. Abingdon: Routledge, 2001.

Seeman, Don. "Otherwise than Meaning: On the Generosity of Ritual." In *Ritual in Its Own Right*, eds. Don Handelman and Galina Lindquist. New York: Berghahn Books, 2005. 55–71.

Shildrick, Margrit. *Embodying the Monster: Encounters with the Vulnerable Self*. London: Sage, 2001.

Siebers, Tobin. "The Return to Ritual: Violence and Art in the Media Age." *Journal for Cultural and Religious Theory* 5/1 (December 2003): 9–33. www.jcrt.org/archives/05.1/siebers.pdf.

Shimazono, Susumu and Margo Kitts. "'Rituals of Death and Remembrance," In *Oxford Handbook of Religion and Violence*, eds. Mark Juergensmeyer, Margo Kitts, and Michael Jerryson. New York: Oxford University Press, 2013. 345–350.

Smith, Gregory A. "How Thin is a Demon?" *Journal of Early Christian Studies* 16/4 (2008):479–512.

Smith, Jonathan Z. *Relating Religion: Essays in the Study of Religion*. Chicago: University of Chicago Press, 2004.

Snoek, Jens, Stausberg, Jan, and Kreinath Michael, eds. *Theorizing Rituals, Vol.1*. Leiden: Brill, 2006.

Sontag, Susan. *Regarding the Pain of Others*. New York: Farrar, Straus, and Giroux, 2003.

Staal, Fritz. "The Meaningless of Ritual." *Numen* 26/1 (1979):2–22.

Stefanini, Rugero. "The Anatolian Origin and Prehistory of the Latin 'Missa' 'Mass'." *Archivio glottologico italiano* 68 (1983):23–49.

Stewart, Pamela and Andrew Strathern, eds. *Violence: Theory and Ethnography*. New York and London: Continuum International Publishing Group, 2002.

Ritual. Farnham: Ashgate, 2010.

Ritual: Key Concepts in Religion. London: Bloomsbury, 2014.

Stone, Jackie. "Relinquishing the Body to Reach the Pure Land." In *Martyrdom, Self-Sacrifice, and Self-Immolation: Religious Perspectives on Suicide*, ed. Margo Kitts. New York: Oxford University Press, 2018. 280–304.

Strathern, Andrew, Pamela Stewart, and Neil Whitehead, eds. *Terror and Violence: Imagination and the Unimaginable*. Ann Arbor: Pluto Press 2006.

Streete, Gail P. "Performing Christian Martyrdoms." In *Martyrdom, Self-Sacrifice, and Self-Immolation: Religious Perspectives on Suicide*, ed. Margo Kitts. New York: Oxford University Press, 2018. 40–53.

Stewart, Pamela and Andrew Strathern. *Witchcraft, Sorcery, Rumors, and Gossip*. New York: Cambridge University Press, 2004.

Tambiah, Stanley J. "The Magic Power of Words," *Man* 3/2 (1968):175–208.

"A Performative Approach to Ritual." *Proceedings of the British Academy*, Vol. 65. Oxford: Oxford University Press, 1979.

Leveling Crowds: Ethnonationalist Conflicts and Collective Violence in South Asia. Berkeley: University of California Press, 1996.

Taussig, Michael. "Culture of Terror, Space of Death: Roger Casement's Putumayo Report and the Explanation of Torture." *Comparative Studies in Society and History* 26:3 (Jul 1984):467–97.

Shamanism, Colonialism, and the Wild Man. Chicago: University of Chicago Press 1987.

Taylor, Charles. "Modern Social Imaginaries." *Public Culture* 14/1 (2002):91–124.

Taylor, Christopher C. *Sacrifice as Terror: The Rwandan Genocide of 1994*. Oxford: Berg Publishers, 1999.

"Genocide and the Religious Imaginary in Rwanda." *Oxford Handbook of Religion and Violence*, eds. Mark Juergensmeyer, Margo Kitts, and Michael Jerryson. New York: Oxford University Press, 2013. 280–292.

Works Cited

Thomas, Julian. "Ritual and Religion in the Neolithic." *Ritual and Religion in the Neolithic*, ed. Timothy Insoll. Oxford: Oxford University Press. 2011/2012 doi: 10.1093/oxfordhb/9780199232444.013.0025.

Thorpe, I. J. N. "Anthropology, Archaeology, and the Origin of Warfare." *World Archaeology* 35/1 (2003):145–165.

Turner, Bryan S. *Regulating Bodies: Essays in Medical Sociology*. London: Routledge, 1992.

Turner, Victor. "Liminal to Liminoid, in Play, Flow and Ritual: An Essay in Comparative Symbology." *Rice Institute Pamphlet – The Rice University Studies* 60/3 (1974):53–92.

"Process, System, and Symbol: A New Anthropological Synthesis." *Daedalus* 106/3 (Summer 1977):61–80.

"Frame, Flow, and Reflection: Ritual and Drama as Public Liminality." *Japanese Journal of Religious Studies* 6/4 (1979):465–499.

Tylor, Edward Burnett. *Religion in Primitive Culture*, Part II, of *Primitive Culture*. New York: Harper and Brothers, 1958 [1871].

Van Gennep, Arnold. *The Rites of Passage*. Chicago: University of Chicago Press [reprint], 1961.

Valeri, Valerio. *Kingship and Sacrifice*. Trans. Paula Wissing. Chicago: University of Chicago Press, 1985.

Vásquez, Manuel A. *More than Belief: A Materialist View of Religion*. New York: Oxford University Press, 2011.

Volkan, Vamik D., Gabriele Ast, and William F. Greer, Jr. *The Third Reich in the Unconscious*. New York: Routledge, 2002.

von Rad, Gerhard. *Holy War in Ancient Israel*, trans. Marva J. Dawn (1958); repr., Grand Rapids: Eerdmans, 1991.

Weinfeld, Moshe. "The Common Heritage of Covenantal Traditions in the Ancient World." In *I Trattai nel mondo antico, forma, ideologica, funzione,* eds. Luciano Canfora, Mario Liverani, and Carlo Zaccagnini. Rome: L'Erinna di Bretschneider, 1990. 175–191.

Whitehead, Neil L. *Dark Shamans: Kanaima and the Poetics of Violent Death.* Durham: Duke University Press, 2002.

"Violence and the Cultural Order." *Daedalus* 136/5 (2007):1–10.

Whitehouse, Harvey. *Modes of Religiosity.* Lanham and Oxford: Altamira Press, 2004.

"Toward an Integration of Ethnography, History, and the Cognitive Science of Religion." In *Religion, Anthropology, and Cognitive Science*, eds. Harvey Whitehouse and James Laidlaw. Durham: Carolina Academic Press, 2007. 247–280.

Vasquez, Manuel. *More than Belief: A Materialist Theory of Religion.* New York: Oxford University Press, 2011.

Visala, Aku and Agustín Fuentes. "Human Nature(s): Human Nature at the Crossroad of Conflicting Interests." *Theology and Science* 13/1 (2015):25–42. doi: 10.1080/14746700.2014.987993.

Wlodarczyk, Nathalie. *Magic and Warfare: Appearance and Reality in Contemporary African Conflict and Beyond.* New York: Palgrave, 2009.

"African Traditional Religion and Violence." In *Oxford Handbook of Religion and Violence*, eds. Mark Juergensmeyer, Margo Kitts, and Michael Jerryson. New York: Oxford University Press, 2013. 153–182.

Xella, Paolo. "'Tophet': An Overall Interpretation." *Studi Epigraphici e Linguistici* 29–30 (2012–2013):259–281.

Yu, Jimmy. *Sanctity and Self-Inflicted Violence in Chinese Religions 1500–1700.* New York: Oxford University Press, 2012.

"Reflections on Self-Immolation in Chinese Buddhist and Daoist Traditions." In *Martyrdom, Self-Sacrifice, and Self-Immolation: Religious Perspectives on Suicide*, ed. Margo Kitts. New York: Oxford University Press, 2018. 264–279.

Cambridge Elements

Religion and Violence

James R. Lewis
University of Tromsø

James R. Lewis is Professor of Religious Studies at the University of
Tromsø, Norway and the author and editor of a number of volumes,
including *The Cambridge Companion to Religion and Terrorism.*

Margo Kitts
Hawai'i Pacific University

Margo Kitts edits the *Journal of Religion and Violence* and is Professor
and Coordinator of Religious Studies and East-West Classical
Studies at Hawai'i Pacific University in Honolulu.

ABOUT THE SERIES:
Violence motivated by religious beliefs has become all too
common in the years since the 9/11 attacks. Not surprisingly,
interest in the topic of religion and violence has grown
substantially since then. This Elements series on Religion and
Violence addresses this new, frontier topic in a series of ca. fifty
individual Elements. Collectively, the volumes will examine a
range of topics, including violence in major world religious
traditions, theories of religion and violence, holy war, witch
hunting, and human sacrifice, among others.

ISSNs: 2397-9496 (online), 2514-3786 (print)

Cambridge Elements ☰

Religion and Violence

Printed in the United States
By Bookmasters